Enjoy the journey of life.

— Regina Richardson

WEALTH MAGNETZ

Foreword by: #1 New York Times
Best Selling author Chérie Carter-Scott, Ph.D

Your A to Z guide for abundant living

REGINA RICHARDSON

All Rights Reserved
© 2009 by Regina Richardson

This book may not be reproduced in whole or in part,
by any means, without written consent of the publisher.

LIFESUCCESS PUBLISHING, LLC
8900 E Pinnacle Peak Road, Suite D240
Scottsdale, AZ 85255
Telephone: 800.473.7134
Fax: 480.661.1014
E-mail: admin@lifesuccesspublishing.com

ISBN: (hard cover) 978-1-59930-197-6
        (e-book)   978-1-59930-278-2

Cover : Dan McElhattan III, m3ad.com & LifeSuccess Publishing
Layout: Fiona Dempsey & LifeSuccess Publishing

COMPANIES, ORGANIZATIONS,
INSTITUTIONS, AND INDUSTRY PUBLICATIONS:
Quantity discounts are available on bulk purchases of this book for reselling,
educational purposes, subscription incentives, gifts,
sponsorship, or fundraising. Special books or book excerpts can also
be created to fit specific needs such as private labeling with your logo
on the cover and a message from a VIP printed inside.
FOR MORE INFORMATION PLEASE CONTACT OUR
SPECIAL SALES DEPARTMENT AT
LIFESUCCESS PUBLISHING.

PRINTED IN CANADA

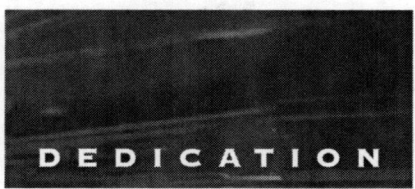

This book is for everyone who dares to believe in him- or herself.

ACKNOWLEDGMENTS

My loving and supportive husband, Gideon. You are the best!

To Gary Elkins for enlightening me on the "knowing" vs. the "knowing about."

Dr. Chérie Carter-Scott, founder of the MMS Institute, author of many insightful and best-selling books, and friend, for coaching me through the process of trusting my own inner guide. You are truly an inspiration.

Rob and Maria Rohe. Thank you for pushing me to be my best and encouraging me to embrace my controller within.

All of the amazing people I've met through PSI Seminars. Thank you for your trust and honesty.

Bob Proctor, of The Secret *and* The Science of Getting Rich *and many other empowering programs, for lighting a spark of desire within me.*

Gerry Robert, author and mentor, for believing in me.

My family, for playing an active role in shaping me into the woman I am today.

Dan and Mary McElhattan, for not giving up on me. Thank you, Dan, for the brilliant book-cover design.

My powerful mastermind group. Thank you for your persistence and support.

All of my friends who have shared their lives with me, thank you for making my world a better place.

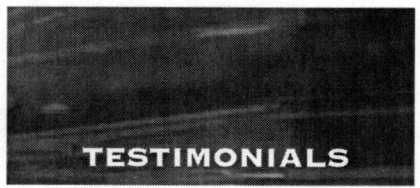

I love the way Regina brought clarity on just how simple accomplishing goals can be!
Mary McElhattan, author of *Rocket Risks,* business coach

Certain laws about wealth and attraction are universal because our Creator masterfully designed it that way. Wealth Magnetz is brilliantly sticky… I was inspired and captivated right from the start.
Adam J. Hathcock, CEO, DFG Development Corporation

Regina Richardson is an inspirational mentor. Now she has shared her secrets of inner motivation and empowerment inside this book. Your life will forever be changed as soon as you start practicing the philosophies found within these pages.
Harry Palmer, financial advisor

We often forget the basic day to day principals and beliefs that will bring us what we want and desire. Wealth Magnetz does a brilliant job of reminding us of the personal actions that we need to take to create riches, of all kinds, in our lives.
Annette Tanori, MA Economics

Regina sets out in her book the essential elements that are required in order to change one's mindset towards wealth and the art of attaining it. To change your circumstances, you must change your thoughts. Regina shows the reader how to do just that.

Todd Dean, author of
More Money Than Month

TABLE OF CONTENTS

Foreword	*13*
Introduction	*15*
Abundance Consciousness	*21*
Beingness	*29*
Creative Thinking	*35*
Determine Your Path	*41*
Emotions Create Your Results	*47*
Freedom to Accept Responsibility	*53*
Givers Gain	*61*
Higher Power	*69*
Intuition	*77*
Joyful Living	*85*
Knowledge	*93*
Lessons	*99*
Being Magnetic = In Alignment	*105*
Now	*111*
Opportunity	*117*
Positive Mental Attitude	*123*
Quality of Life	*129*
Relationships	*137*
Success	*143*
Time	*149*
Understanding	*155*
Vibration	*161*
Will	*167*
The X Factor	*173*
You Have All You Need	*179*
Zeal	*187*
Start Here, Start Now	*193*

FOREWORD

Most of us grow up with a myopic perspective on life. We have a family that may be blissful or dysfunctional, but that microcosm of life is what we experience as our world. When we venture out into the social network of people and organizations, we receive feedback about our behavior. It is at this point that we start to see ourselves in relation to others. When you look in the mirror of another person, you have options. You can appreciate what you see; you can judge what you perceive; you can question what you observe; or you can grow from what you discover.

Although wealth comes in many forms, for most people, money directly equates with wealth. One's relationship to money is one of the myopic areas for growth. You may be a hoarder, a squanderer, an investor, or simply allergic to money. Investigating your relationship to money is a worthwhile activity, regardless of what you discover. Money is a form of energy that must be addressed if you are going to live in the world of producing and consuming. Not having, having some, having a lot, or having an abundance of wealth is directly related to one's concept of self-esteem, sense of deserving, and one's capacity for abundance. Examining what you believe, what you feel, and what thoughts you harbor in relation to having money will expand your consciousness and your capacity to allow wealth to magnetize to you.

Regina Richardson has worked through many of her limiting beliefs regarding her relationship to having an abundance of money. In *Wealth Magnetz*, Regina reaches out to help you through any past baggage that you may have acquired in relation to money. Her objective is to liberate you from the poverty-consciousness chains that could keep you from attracting all the abundance you deserve. Regina wants everyone to experience the joys she has discovered, and she will hold your hand along the journey from scarcity to abundance to becoming a human wealth magnet.

Chérie Carter-Scott, Ph.D.
author of *If Life Is a Game,*
These are the Rules: Ten Rules for Being Human

INTRODUCTION

During my formative years, my family didn't have much money. In fact, we hardly had enough money to pay the rent and stay fed. We never were starving, although we would live off of beans and tortillas for a week at a time. My father worked, and my mother was a stay-at-home mom. My father made a decent amount of money; however, my family always spent more than we had. My parents were always stressed about credit-card bills and the bank account having a negative sign in front of the balance.

Going shopping for school clothes was always a stressful time. We'd have to go to outlet stores and look for the sales. My mom was always worried about spending too much, and at the same time, she wanted to be able to give us what we needed. To this day, I feel tense when I go shopping and have to remind myself I am wealthy and don't need to feel stressed. It sounds ridiculous, but it's true.

I got my first summer job at the age of fourteen. I wanted to have my own money and take the pressure off of my parents to provide for the frivolous things I wanted. I felt rich and liked the feeling of being able to pay for what I wanted instead of what was on sale. Before I knew it, though, the money I earned was gone. The habit of spending before you make it was already ingrained in me. My sister took the opposite approach. She would act like a miser and hold onto every cent she earned. It seemed like it pained her to let go of money. Both of us had the belief system about money instilled in us that there is never enough; we just displayed it from opposite ends of the spectrum.

When I was quite young, I made a vow to myself to always make my own money and be able to take care of myself. Throughout the years, I've done just that. However, it wasn't until I started looking at my belief system and philosophy about money that I realized why I still didn't have a lot of extra when it came to my finances. I was able to do most of the things I wanted to do, but I didn't consider myself wealthy or rich by any means. Wealthy people were lucky, or born into privilege, or smarter than I was. Through implementing the various processes of my mentors—such as Bob Proctor, Dr. Cherie Carter-Scott, Mark Victor Hansen, Jerry and Esther Hicks (The Teachings of Abraham), and Dr. John Demartini—I was able to shift my limiting thought processes in regard to wealth.

You may have already heard some of the concepts I share in this book. Repetition is one of the ways we learn. Knowing about the principles of creating wealth is much different than practicing them. I urge you to read this material with new eyes and listen with new ears. Maybe this time you will hear something in such a way that it causes you to take action. *Wealth Magnetz* is designed for you to put into practice what you already know. It is my intent to share with you easy-to-follow steps that will guide you in shifting your mindset from knowing about wealth-building concepts to gaining a truer understanding or knowing through experience. And by doing so, you will create an amazing life full of wealth, abundance, and liberty.

Close your eyes and imagine what it would be like to be wealthy. Did you imagine a big house, nice cars, or a lounge chair under a palm tree on a beach? If you were to ask one hundred people what wealth is, you'd probably get one hundred different answers. Wealth is not an absolute accomplishment that can be checked off a list. There's no widely agreed-upon definition, and therefore it's up to you to decide what it means and when you have achieved it. Other people's ideas of what wealth is simply don't matter. You may hear the concept of wealth described as many things—including money, friendships, relationships, health, the quantity of possessions, the quality of possessions, inner peace, or any combination of these ideas.

INTRODUCTION

However, when you closed your eyes and thought about living a wealthy life, did you imagine a big pile of cash? Most people don't—they focus on the emotion and wonderful feelings they imagine wealth will bring. It is important to understand that money is not wealth. It is a medium of exchange that allows you to live a wealthy life. This may seem like a small bit of difference, but it is very important. The ability to attract money into your life is what allows you to live as you choose and have what you desire. It is this type of wealth that *Wealth Magnetz* will help you attract—not cash for the sake of cash, but money to allow you to live your purpose and passion.

At what point will you call yourself wealthy? And what will allow you to live the life of your dreams? To be able to go where you want to go and do what you want to do when you want to is nothing less than true liberty. You may have a very successful career or business, but that doesn't mean you have the time to go on a family vacation with the people you love the most when they want to go. It is possible to create financial wealth and have liberty at the same time, but it can only happen when you know and define exactly what you want and take the steps necessary to get it.

> *Step back and evaluate where your beliefs about money and wealth originated.*

Before you can start your journey to wealth, you must first acknowledge where you are in life and how you got there. This means being brutally honest with yourself and accepting responsibility for your choices and perceived mistakes. It also means you must take a step back and evaluate where your beliefs about money and wealth originated. Understand this is not an opportunity to beat yourself up over the past. The past can't be changed and nothing can be gained by pouring more negative emotion into those events. I encourage you to take a non-emotional look at the reality of your situation and what actions brought it about.

This is not easy for anyone. As human beings, we only like to do what feels good, but it is important to let go of the emotions surrounding the past and look at the choices you can now make to shape your future. You can think of this as doing what will feel good tomorrow. When you are presented with a choice, think about how you will feel about it tomorrow or next week or next year and choose the direction you know will produce those positive feelings.

I don't mean to imply that these new choices will be easy. It can feel awkward and uncomfortable to create new habits and incorporate new ideas into your life. However, the sense of empowerment you will gain by taking control and making conscious and active choices, rather than just taking the easiest or most familiar options, will give you a great sense of accomplishment. A week, month, or year from now, you will be able to look back at those choices and know they made a positive difference in your life. You will no longer feel badly or ashamed about how you came to be in your present circumstance. This great sense of control over your life gives the additional motivation to keep making good choices that will lead to the wealth and liberty you deserve.

This is not to insinuate that all or even some of your choices have been bad. You may be relatively happy with your life but just want more freedom and fulfillment. As you assess your previous choices, pat yourself on the back for the things you've already accomplished. It is human nature for us to remember bad choices for months or even years and almost immediately forget the good choices and daily miracles that occur in our lives. A good practice is to write down what's going well and remind yourself how many good things happen in your life each day.

Once you've honestly assessed where you are in your life and how you got here, it's time to start dreaming again. Really dream. Don't reject thoughts that come to mind as impossible or impractical—write down everything your heart desires, even if it seems far-fetched and you have no idea how it will be accomplished. Without big dreams, you cannot catapult yourself up the ladder of success.

INTRODUCTION

Once you decide what your idea of a wealthy life is, you can then decide what you will use the money for. Is it to be able to spend time with your family? Is it to be able to help others who are less fortunate? Is it to pursue your dream business? Once you write down what your dreams are—and be specific—then it becomes relatively easy to assign a dollar figure to the amount of money it will take to achieve them. Money or wealth—as abstract ideas—aren't motivating, nor do they inspire you to action. It is only when you know what wealth means for you and you can imagine yourself having that life that it motivates you to take action to achieve it. Having a specific and definable dream allows you to direct your thoughts toward something concrete rather than just an abstract idea.

After you have an amount of money in mind, it's time to create a plan and take action to achieve it. An important part of making any type of plan is to write it down. This means you write down the big dreams (such as owning your own real-estate investment business) and the small ones (like taking the whole family on a cruise to the Caribbean). It can also include items such as reducing your weight by thirty pounds or becoming healthier by exercising three times per week. Once you have these items written down, then you start setting daily, weekly, and monthly goals to accomplish them. Write these down too, so you can track your progress.

By using the principles outlined in Wealth Magnetz, *you can achieve anything you desire.*

Now it's time for action. By using the principles outlined in *Wealth Magnetz*, you can achieve anything you desire. I challenge you to make a commitment (actually put it in writing) to practice the *Wealth Magnetz* principles described in each chapter for thirty days. You can start small with only one or two at first, and then you can incorporate more as you see the results.

The first thing to put into practice is affirmations. Kinesiology proves the importance of what we say to ourselves. We can strengthen our bodies or tear them down with our thoughts and words. There is a positive affirmation for each chapter subject. You may use the affirmations provided or create your own. Make sure you start each affirmation with the words "I am," and you must write them as if you already are or have whatever it is you want. Speak your affirmations several times a day. Make a list of all of them to keep on your bathroom mirror as a reminder.

Tracking your progress is an essential part of the process because we tend to remember our setbacks and failures longer than we do our successes. By tracking your progress, you can easily see how many successes you have had and how they tremendously outweigh the occasional setback. Writing things down also alerts you to those times when you may be losing focus or getting off track and will help you to quickly realign your actions with what you want.

There is no one secret to getting what you want out of life, but there are thousands of ways to hold yourself back and be miserable. Through honest self-assessment and a desire to be, do, and have more in your life, you can change any circumstance—no matter how bad—and live a life of your choosing. So many people take the attitude that life happens to them and they just accept what is offered—never daring to even think that they can take an active role in shaping events that affect them. I urge you to understand the innate power each person possesses and harness that power within you to create your new, wealthy life.

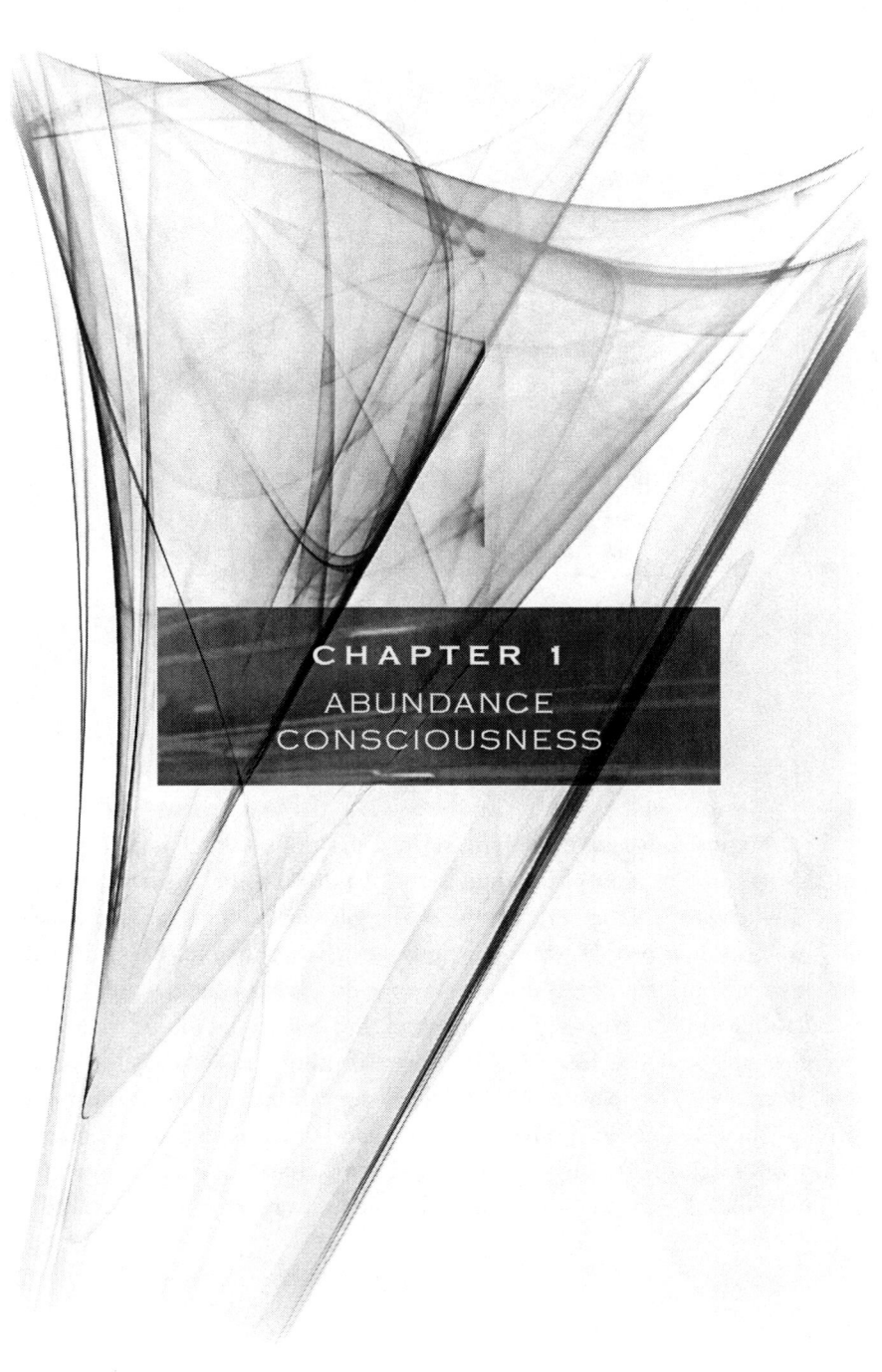

CHAPTER 1
ABUNDANCE CONSCIOUSNESS

CHAPTER 1

ABUNDANCE CONSCIOUSNESS

I welcome all the abundance life has in store for me.

Your overall attitude and perception of life is what is called your consciousness. You don't really think about it; it is just part of you. For example, do you know people who are largely negative in their thinking and always see the glass as half empty? Conversely, do you also know people who are largely positive in their thinking and see challenges as opportunities? You have a specific consciousness which reveals if you think life is a great big struggle and you must scratch and claw your way through, or if you feel that life is a welcoming and rewarding journey. Most people who live paycheck to paycheck are exhibiting a consciousness of scarcity. They always fear not having enough and want more but are skeptical if they will receive it. The idea of abundance consciousness is you know there is enough for all, and you are convinced more is always coming your way.

CHAPTER 1
ABUNDANCE CONSCIOUSNESS

Most people's ideas about money are formed when they are young. For example, if you had a parent that always said, "We can't afford that," then it is natural to grow up and perceive that everything you want is very expensive and therefore you can't have it. In another situation, if someone has grown up with a parent who used money as a substitute for meeting his emotional needs, he can then develop a very unhealthy relationship with money, which can lead to poor financial decisions that don't serve him.

If you catch yourself constantly saying things are too expensive or they are out of your price range, it is important to understand why you are saying it. Is it because you've lost your job and have dust bunnies in your bank account, or is it something else? By that, I mean, do you think you would feel uncomfortable owning nice things or living in a particular neighborhood? It may sound odd to some, but many people have peculiar perceptions about what it means to have abundance or wealth.

Shirley came from a lower-middle-class background. She did very well in sales, and one day she treated herself to a very expensive blouse. She took it home and it hung in her closet for weeks. She would look at it every day but then choose something else to wear. She just didn't feel comfortable or worthy to wear something that expensive. This was completely her perception as she could easily afford the blouse and had earned it. It was not until Shirley let go of her own limiting beliefs and embraced the mindset of abundance that she was able to wear the blouse.

She just didn't feel comfortable or worthy to wear something that expensive.

The concept of abundance is the understanding that there is enough to go around. If you take a breath, does that mean there is less air? Of course not! Wealth works in this same way. If you choose to make more money, or even become a millionaire, does that mean there is less money for others? No, it doesn't. In fact, it really means there is more. As you receive abundance, it is important to allow it to flow through you. It must circulate, which means you then get to improve the lives of others and those you love as more abundance comes into your life.

AFFIRMATION
I WELCOME ALL THE ABUNDANCE LIFE HAS IN STORE FOR ME.

You may notice as you work to transform your thinking into abundance consciousness that you become aware of a lot of people around you who have a poverty mindset. There are undoubtedly some who will comment on how you have become so free with your cash. This happened to me at lunch with some friends. Not only did I treat them, but one of my friends commented about the large tip I left. I see this big tipping as my way of giving to the universe as I know what I freely give will be freely returned to me. I told my friend this but only got a skeptical laugh as she said, "With that attitude, you'll be broke in a year."

At first I was a little annoyed, but then I realized this friend (who is an avid coupon clipper) is constantly trying to find the best bargain and save five or ten cents at every turn rather than focusing on bringing wealth into her life. I know her life is one of constant worry and struggle, whereas mine has now become one of peace. I don't have to worry about a dollar here or there because I've let go of the worry that I might not get that money back. I know I will, and therefore I can sleep easily at night.

And then there are your parents. Some of the most difficult, limiting beliefs to overcome—especially concerning financial matters—are those shared by close family members. This is due to the fact you all share the same socio-economic background and similar experiences. We all want to belong to a group, and this keeps us within a certain comfort zone. Anyone trying to move out of the accepted norms is seen as a threat and the family will try to pull him back into what is comfortable. This is why we have clichés such as the following:

Don't get above your raising.

Champagne taste on a beer budget.

A fool and his money are soon parted.

Money is the root of all evil.

These negative and skeptical views are passed down from generation to generation and can create an environment where any family member who yearns for more from life is seen as someone who can't be satisfied or wants more than he deserves. The sad part is this thinking becomes embedded in our minds and affects how we think about money and what the possession of certain things says about us.

I find it interesting that as I have moved into an abundance consciousness, I seem to encounter more people who live in a poverty mindset. These are not poor people, but they are people of middle- to upper-middle-class incomes. But they think about money as if they are almost destitute.

For example, the friend I previously mentioned as a coupon clipper not only scrimps on groceries and dinners out, but she will also drive all over town to save three cents on a gallon of gasoline. When you think about it, if your car holds twenty gallons of gas, the savings of three cents is only sixty cents per fill up. I confronted her with this fact a short time ago and asked if all that running around to save sixty cents was worth it. She said, "Of course it is. It makes me feel like I'm making the most of my money and not wasting anything." Clearly, in my mind, she is wasting something—her time. I grew up near this friend and know her parents watched every dime. As a child, she was praised more for saving money than for getting good grades, and that has obviously carried over into adulthood.

> *As a child, she was praised more for saving money than for getting good grades.*

While this may seem like irrational behavior to some, we all have hang-ups about money and occasionally behave in a manner that doesn't make sense in accordance to the beliefs we were raised with. Think about those friends or people you know who spend their time and energy trying to win the lottery or making a million in Vegas. Many people have the attitude that monetary wealth is something to be attained overnight and is not a result of an ongoing mindset of abundance, followed with action over a period of time. I always wonder how much these people might have accumulated over the past twenty years if they had invested that lottery money in wealth-building seminars to change their thinking. Not surprisingly, most of the people I know who try to hit it big have never gained one darned thing.

Not all of my friends believe and live with this poverty mindset. As I have grown and learned how to bring wealth and abundance into my life, I've also gained new friends who have the same mindset of abundance. There is something to be said for living and acting with this mindset, and early on in our friendship, one friend and I would try it out. When we went on trips or out to dinners, we acted as if we really were wealthy, and much to our surprise people treated us as though we were. There were times in which it truly was an act, and both of us were struggling to pay off our credit-card bills every month. Being able to gain entry into the worlds of symphonies, charity balls, and travel gave us a taste of what life could offer and how easily it could be attained. There were numerous times we would glance over at one another and ask, "How did we get here?" The whole idea is it allowed us to put our financial concerns into proper perspective and realize we could and would pay our bills while still remembering the taste of the life we wanted to eventually lead.

Many self-help gurus tout the idea that if you can imagine living a certain life, it is much more likely you will attain it. My experience is if you can actually touch, taste, and feel that world, then your motivation skyrockets, and you will move heaven and earth to meet your goals. For example, if you dream of living in a villa on the coast of Italy, then use some of your money to take a trip there. Take pictures, wiggle your toes in the Mediterranean, and walk among the ancient ruins. Watch the sunset and breathe the air. When you arrive home, your mind will easily be able to imagine living a life in that environment because you have been there, even if only for a brief moment.

Early on, when I was just getting used to the idea of an abundance consciousness, I went to dinner with a friend who was already well versed in the concept. He chose a very expensive restaurant, and when I looked at the price of the steaks on the menu, my first thought was that there had

CHAPTER 1
ABUNDANCE CONSCIOUSNESS

better be a whole cow attached. And of course, all the sides were a la carte. I was shocked and very worried he may not have realized how expensive the restaurant was when he booked the reservation. I leaned over and asked, "Why would someone pay seventy-five dollars for just a steak?" He smiled and said, "You do—because that is what it costs, and you have it." I sat for a minute and realized he was right. I did have it. I belonged there just like anyone else. I calmed immediately and thoroughly enjoyed the rest of the dinner.

While eating a seventy-five-dollar steak may not be something I do every day, I've learned that living my dream brings wonderful, positive emotions that motivate and encourage me. It also attracts the people and events that help me improve my life and bring me wealth. Once you begin acting as if you have a life of abundance, you will have a life of abundance. This comes more from your attitude.

There are some behaviors that highlight your own limiting beliefs about money and reinforce a poverty mindset. See if any of these look familiar:

Clipping coupons

Shopping at discount or wholesale stores

Scanning the sales circulars and only buying items on sale

Driving around to save a few cents on a gallon of gasoline

Presenting restaurant coupons for free desserts or two-for-one specials

I'm not saying being aware of your money and where it goes is a bad thing, but hoarding your funds indicates a sense of scarcity and lacking—much like Ebenezer Scrooge. If you recall the story, the lesson wasn't in the spending of money; it was in the giving of oneself—in other words, living abundantly in every way.

AFFIRMATION
I WELCOME ALL THE ABUNDANCE LIFE HAS IN STORE FOR ME.

Money is just as abundant as air, and yet many hold onto it as if it has all been allocated to the special or worthy—and any they get is by chance. In order to get what you want and pursue your dreams, you must first be willing to let go of what you have. It is not possible to have a scarcity consciousness and be able to let abundance in.

Now I'd like for you to think of what you really want out of life. Allow yourself to dream as you did when you were a child. Don't worry about how it will happen; just let your thoughts flow. Whatever your dream is for your life, you can achieve it. You can attract money, wealth, friends, or whatever you desire if you choose to live with an abundance consciousness. I challenge you right now to set aside all of those beliefs that stand in your way and take the first step to a new and fabulous life.

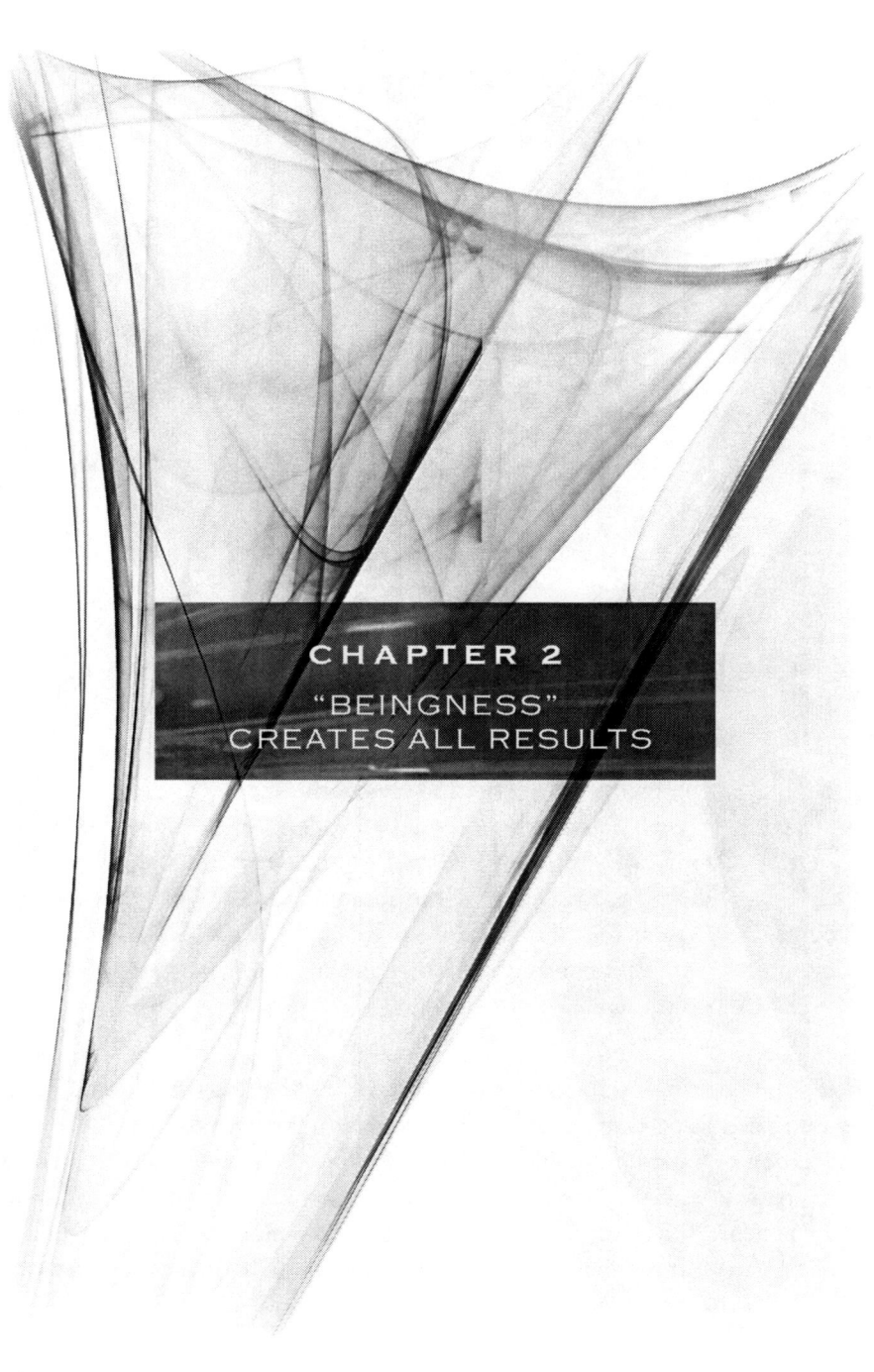

CHAPTER 2
"BEINGNESS" CREATES ALL RESULTS

CHAPTER 2

"BEINGNESS" CREATES ALL RESULTS

I am grateful for attracting wealth.

Many of us have been in situations where we felt battered by life. You may have thought life wasn't fair, or it was not your fault, and wondered why things were so hard. Each and every one of us has the ability to choose how we view the circumstances in our life. We decide if we are happy or sad, loving or angry. Circumstances appear on a daily basis that give us the opportunity to choose how we will be. This is called our "beingness."

Beingness is defined as the emotions underneath or behind our actions. Have you ever experienced someone being patient with you, yet also felt his or her frustration or anger underneath? Conversely, have you experienced someone being patient with you, yet also felt their love and care for you driving them to be patient? The result in both situations was patience, and yet two different feelings or emotions were created because of the beingness behind the action.

CHAPTER 2
"BEINGNESS" CREATES ALL RESULTS

We have the power as human beings to generate whatever beingness we want. We can choose how we feel about anything. Instead of reacting to any outside stimuli, we have the power of controlling our own emotions. I have a friend whose boyfriend and the father of her child just broke up with her. He had not wanted her to work and had been taking care of her financially, however he was never there for her on an emotional level. She has had to leave her beautiful home and lifestyle—without a job or a vehicle—and must live with family until she gets on her feet. Many people would be depressed by having to live under those circumstances. However, she has chosen to be happy and to create what she wants and deserves. Within just a short couple of weeks, she has already attracted a great career and new friends who are like-minded and uplifting. She was able to do this because of her being joyful, powerful, and grateful—under even the worst circumstances.

Truly living your beingness also means living in the present. You cannot harbor resentments or fears that would encourage you to attach unwarranted emotion to a given situation. This can be very common in our relationships with others. If someone close to you has hurt you, it is easy to become distrustful. You choose to distrust those who try to have a relationship with you and therefore miss out on what they may have to offer. Current events are not seen in the clear light of the present; they are clouded by the past.

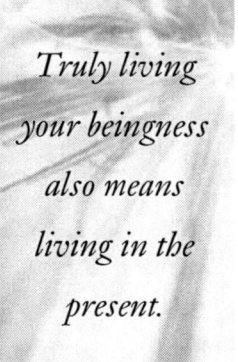

Truly living your beingness also means living in the present.

This can also happen in our relationship with money. Some are so focused on the future that they don't enjoy today. They constantly make statements that are something like: "I'll be happy when …" They never choose to be happy today. Choosing means taking responsibility for your emotions, your behaviors and actions, and therefore your results.

You will not attain wealth without being completely and totally responsible for your results. If you could, you would already be wealthy. If you are the

AFFIRMATION
I AM GRATEFUL FOR ATTRACTING WEALTH.

type of person who is living paycheck to paycheck or even getting by comfortably but not really getting ahead, then you will not change your results until you accept the present.

I have an acquaintance, let's call him Kenny, who is always chasing that next moneymaking idea. He's in terrible financial shape and even had to declare bankruptcy, but he's still certain the next idea will work and keeps trying. While I commend Kenny's persistence, when you really talk to him, you understand why nothing ever works. The conversation usually goes something like this:

"Hey, Kenny. What about that restaurant you were going to open?"

"Well, the bank had too many requirements. It's almost like they don't want people to go into business anymore; it really is sad."

"Well, what about that paintless, dent-repair shop you and Ron were going to open?"

"Ron's wife wasn't on board with it and kept insisting he couldn't quit his regular job. I'm sure glad I don't have a wife who controls me like that."

"Didn't you say you and Tony were going to try your hand at building fences for people this summer?"

"Yeah, we're gonna do that, but there's four of us and we can't all seem to get together at one time and get the legal paperwork going. But we can still do your fence if you want. We'll just do it on the side, and I'll give you a real good deal."

Some people want to look outside of themselves for excuses and reasons for their life being less than they want. Actually, they are caught up in reacting to external events rather than realizing they have the power to perceive those events differently. If you think about it, making excuses and blaming events

CHAPTER 2
"BEINGNESS" CREATES ALL RESULTS

outside yourself keeps you living a victimized life. By stepping up and taking responsibility, you declare you are going to get something done, no matter what obstacles come in your way.

Emotions have the capacity to harness huge amounts of energy. The energy from those emotions can either be used to enhance or hinder your forward progress. You may discover you are using large amounts of energy to defend a denial system that is not serving you. This denial system will only allow you to develop limiting beliefs and behaviors.

One of the first steps in changing your beingness is to become aware of your own limiting behaviors. You must confront the belief system that is blocking your success and begin practicing new behaviors to empower yourself. If you allow yourself the opportunity to get in touch with your beingness, then you will see the emotions underlying the issues and incorrect perceptions in many areas of your life. This understanding will allow you to recognize when your emotions take control and give you the opportunity to choose to change your ineffective behaviors on the spot. You can then go back and analyze the event and find out which limiting belief was at work and address it.

Emotional intelligence (EI), a phrase made famous by Daniel Goleman, author of many books on the subject, begins with self-awareness and self-management. Goleman writes that in high-emotional states, we often get "hijacked" by the power of our feelings, but we can learn to catch ourselves and direct our emotions before they direct us.

> *In high-emotional states, we often get "hijacked" by the power of our feelings, but we can learn to catch ourselves and direct our emotions before they direct us.*

When Ryan graduated college, his family decided to take a cruise in the Caribbean. Ryan at first said no, that he "wasn't really a water person." The idea made him nervous, and he'd never liked to swim. He thought about where the emotion stemmed from and remembered an incident when he was first taking swim lessons and had gone underwater and panicked. He had avoided the water ever since.

After considering the source of his nervousness regarding water, Ryan chose to go on the cruise and confront his fears. He waded into the ocean and even went parasailing. He never even realized all the things he allowed his fear to keep him from enjoying. Just choosing to investigate the source of one small, limiting belief can open your life to new and fabulous possibilities.

The idea of getting in touch with your beingness is not about wanting to get rid of your emotions. Emotions are good and are often the only indicator you may have of an area in your life that needs work. Emotions can and will happen. Allow yourself to feel them and stay in control of them rather than letting your emotions control you. By gaining awareness in the heat of the moment, you will become more practiced at managing all of your emotional energy with intention and purpose to achieve what you really want in life.

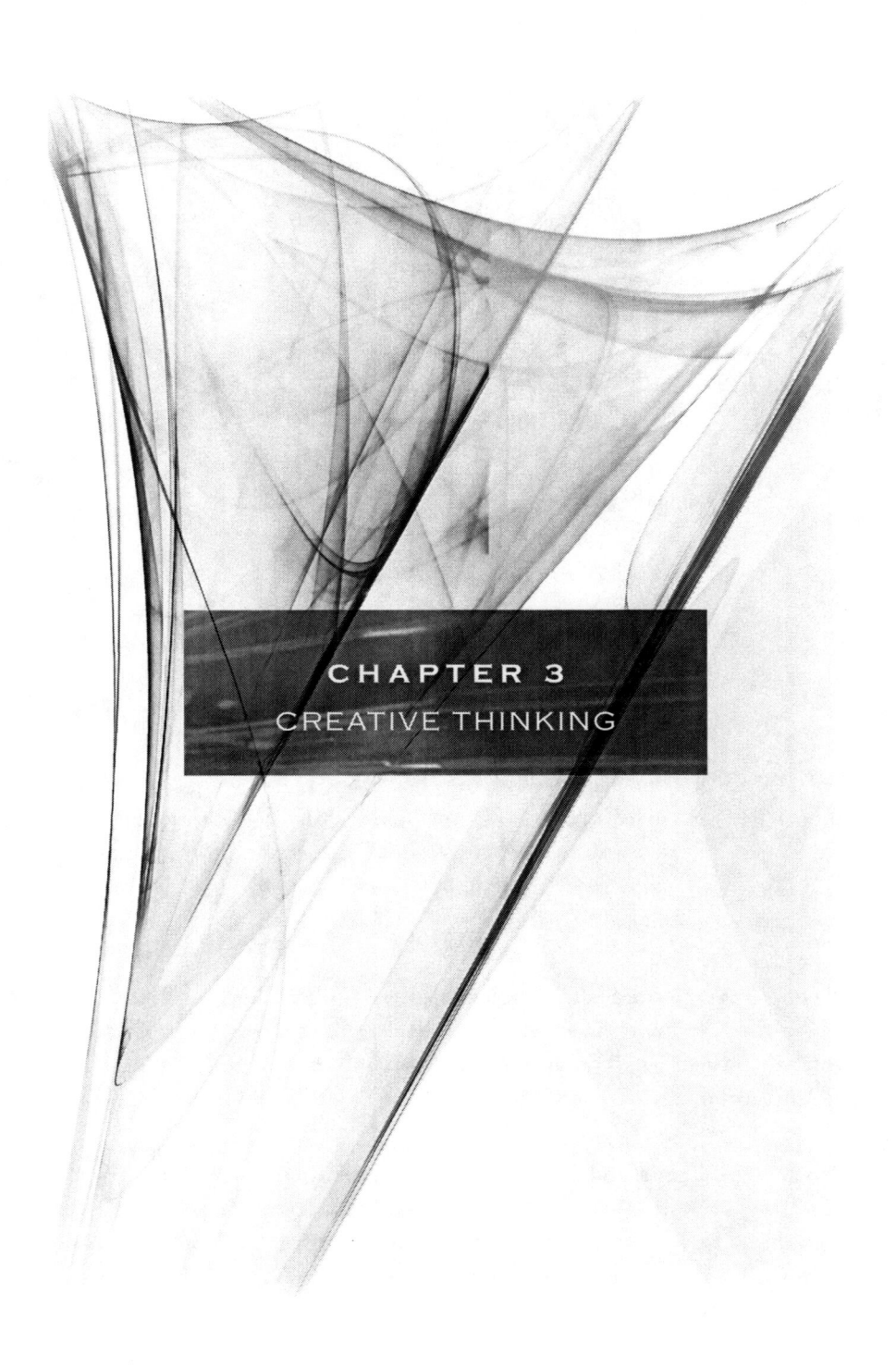

CHAPTER 3
CREATIVE THINKING

CHAPTER 3

CREATIVE THINKING

I am a creative genius.

Whenever you set a big goal, you may find yourself faced with what appear to be major obstacles. It is important at this time to remember to focus on how you can instead of why you can't do or have something. When you use creative thinking, you are solution oriented.

Have you ever noticed, after you have successfully achieved a goal, that most of the obstacles in getting it were only perceived as such in your mind when you first started? We have an inner critic telling us why we can't, shouldn't, or don't deserve.

When my husband and I were dating, we took a trip to Europe. He was expecting money from his first, big real-estate deal to be wired into his bank account while we were there. He knew the money was coming and wanted to impress me by staying in one of the finest hotels in Venice and taking me on an Italian shopping extravaganza. Days and weeks went by and no money arrived in his account. The balances on our credit cards were climbing, and he started to worry and stress about how he was going to cover the hotel bill as well as take us shopping. We had to keep finding solutions to be able to pay for our stay on a daily basis.

When the money finally came in, there were issues getting it transferred to an account we could use overseas. It could have been a nightmare. However, we kept finding creative solution after solution because we were sure the money would eventually come. Our focus was on the outcome we wanted, not on all the perceived obstacles. We ended up having one of the most amazing vacations ever.

You are a creative genius whether you feel like it or not. All you have to do is start flexing your creative muscle. Whatever you goal is, start thinking of ways to achieve it. Even if the first solution that comes to mind sounds a bit ridiculous, keep focusing on creating solutions until the right one comes to you. And, when you are sure a solution will come, it will. No matter what you think, you are right. What do you choose to be right about? The obstacle or the solution to getting your goal?

We are each born as creative beings, and creativity can be enhanced and learned. Sometimes, creative thinking requires us to look at things from new perspectives. Creativity is also a state of mind. If you constantly tell yourself or others, "I'm not very creative," or "I can never come up with good ideas," then it causes your own, innate creative ability to atrophy. Creative thinking requires positive thinking.

A positive atmosphere contributes to a positive and creative state of mind. Some people thrive in loud, people-filled areas with much activity and are drawn to large cities such as New York. Others need quiet and calm to think clearly and crave the peace and serenity of nature. This is not about daydreaming or letting your mind merely wander. It is about focusing on your goal and finding as many creative ways as possible to reach it.

AFFIRMATION
I AM A CREATIVE GENIUS.

For example, let's assume you want to buy a new home, and the home you like, you perceive to be a little out of your price range. The old you may have thought, "Well, there's no way," and left it at that. But now you know you choose—so you choose to focus on the goal of your dream home and think creatively about ways it can be yours. You may enlist others in the process as well, such as others who have purchased homes creatively or your realtor. They may know of solutions you've never even thought about, but your dream won't happen if you squash the idea from the outset and never look for a solution.

Creativity isn't about dreaming up something that isn't there. It's about seeing solutions that already exist which you can't see right now. Sound crazy? Have you ever gone to purchase a car and thought, "Hey, I'll get a bright blue one; almost no one has a car like this." The minute you drive it off the lot, you will begin to see bright blue cars everywhere you turn. In fact, it may seem as if the entire world just went out and bought cars just like yours. In reality, the cars were always there, but you just didn't see them. A blue car hadn't been brought to a conscious awareness within your mind.

This is the same thing that happens when you start to look for creative solutions to issues in your life. The solutions present themselves as if by magic. Actually, they have always existed and may even have come tapping at your door previously, but you weren't aware of the need, so you ignored them.

Harnessing your own creativity to find what works for you takes patience and practice. You can start by doing the following things:

1. Become Aware: Are there areas of your life that seem to be going nowhere? Take a look at the real reasons and choose to focus on a goal to put you in a better circumstance. Once you become aware of your past negative thoughts and actions, you can start to make changes that move you toward your goal instead of away from it.

CHAPTER 3
CREATIVE THINKING

2. Stay Open to Possibilities: If you come up with one solution, don't limit yourself. Often, those who are a little new to this creativity will find one solution and then stop. They fall back into their old way of thinking and assume that to be the only solution. Creativity takes practice, and as you learn to see all the options, more will open themselves to you.

3. Get Back on Track: Everyone gets a little off track on occasion and loses sight of their goal. Don't let that convince you that you don't deserve to get what you want. Just get back on course, and you will again start seeing the solutions you have missed or overlooked.

4. Positive Is as Positive Does: If you are constantly surrounded by friends and family whose conversations drip with negativity, you may want to add some new friends or associates who think as you do. While we can't change others, we can change ourselves—and choosing to immerse yourself in negativity while you are making the transition can make it extremely difficult. Once you get the hang of a positive outlook, you will be able to protect yourself from being dragged down by the negative attitude of others.

You can let go of the pressing concerns of the day and interject a small amount of time for peaceful contemplation.

5. Be Determined: Creativity takes practice. Your creativity is there within you, but you must make a habit of using your imagination. Before you give up or decide this is not for you, give it a valid shot—not the half-hearted try you may have given your last diet. Do it like your life depends on the outcome, and you will be shocked and amazed at the changes in your life. Although many of your best ideas will come when you aren't really concentrating, you can make them happen more often by regularly seeking new ideas and solutions to the challenges before you.

6. Schedule a Time: Even if you're not plotting how to earn your next million dollars, set aside a certain amount of time each day, week, or month to relax, brainstorm new ideas, and think about what might come next for you. Make creative thinking a habit. By regularly scheduling a time to relax and focus, you can let go of the pressing concerns of the day and interject a small amount of time for peaceful contemplation.

7. There Are No Bad Ideas: Keep a file or notebook of your ideas. This can be a very valuable tool, not only now, but in the future. While you might not act on a specific idea or solution today, next month or next year you may be facing an issue for which it is the perfect solution. There are times when you may feel stuck as if your well of creative ideas has sprung a big, fat leak. This is the perfect time to read back through your notebook of old ideas and see if one of them sparks a new solution.

Creativity can be used in a myriad of ways, from enhancing your wealth to improving the quality of your relationships. The same tools that help you figure out how to create the next wonderful invention or service will lead you to the people that can help you. Once you have mastered the basic tools, you will be astounded at how your eyes are opened to the possibilities existing all around you right now.

CHAPTER 4
DETERMINE YOUR PATH

CHAPTER 4

DETERMINE YOUR PATH

I am clear on what it is I want.

In the story of the Wizard of Oz, Dorothy finds herself somewhere over the rainbow. She desperately wants to go back home, and her only possibility is to go see the wizard in the city of Oz. In order to get there she has to follow the yellow brick road. Along the road, she encountered several obstacles. However, she did not let anything stop her from going where she wanted to go. Dorothy could have decided the flying monkeys were too scary and turned around to stay with the munchkins. But she didn't. She was set on making it to the wizard so she could get home. And she got her goal. She knew exactly what she wanted.

In your mind, what does your end result look like to you? Once you are clear on what it is you want, then you can set your path to follow. Setting a specific goal will support you in knowing your path. Let's say you want to make a million dollars in a year. How do you want to make it? You can make it with one idea (such as a patented product), you can work in your current business (sales- or commission-producing jobs), or you may have multiple sources of income. There are many ways to make money.

Many people stop listening when I mention one million dollars. (If that figure is too low for you, substitute it with your desired amount.) But let's look at that amount in a realistic and doable way.

The first step is to punch the total amount you want to make into the calculator: $1,000,000. Then take that figure and divide it by twelve months—which is $83,333. This is the amount you must produce each and every month for one year to reach your goal. Now take this new amount and divide it by 4.3—which is the average number of weeks per month. This brings the new weekly total to about $19,380. This is the amount you must earn on a weekly basis to make one million dollars per year.

Now let's suppose that you are thinking of a new product or service you can sell for ninety-nine dollars. You would take the weekly amount and divide it by the price of this new service. This comes to 195. You have to sell 195 units of this new service each week to make one million dollars per year. That's less than twenty-eight per day. You only have to get twenty-eight people every day to buy your product to make one million dollars per year.

THE ONLY QUESTION at this point is what new service you could provide that gives enough value to be worth ninety-nine dollars or more to people. You can start with something like the following list:

1. Training program (CD set) to show people how to be wealthy: $99

2. Seminar to teach the same program live: $299

3. Book to complement the program: $30

YOU WOULD THEN set your goals for each day. They might look something like this:

AFFIRMATION
I AM CLEAR ON WHAT IT IS I WANT.

> I will sell 28 $99 How to be Wealthy CDs (Basic Course)
>
> I will sell 6 $299 seminar tickets each day
>
> I will sell 33 $30 books per day

IT DOESN'T SOUND like much, does it? In fact, you may be thinking you could do much more. And you easily could. But let's assume you just started here and met your goal each day. Do you know how much you'd have at the end of one year: over two million dollars. Even if you just met your goal every other day, it would still be more than one million dollars. By breaking down the goal into monthly, weekly, then daily goals, it becomes much easier for the mind to grasp—it becomes really doable and allows you to focus on a daily goal rather than be overwhelmed by the one-million-dollar idea.

A great system I follow is called the SMART goal system. SMART stands for:

> Specific: The most important thing for you to set your path is to know exactly what it is you want.
>
> Measurable: Make it a tangible goal (something you can see, feel, touch).
>
> Attainable: Something possible for you to get (i.e., if you are a forty-year-old woman, you would not set a goal of playing in the NFL).
>
> Risky: The kind of goal you may feel nauseous about when you state it aloud because it really stretches your idea of what is possible.
>
> Time: A goal is a dream with a deadline. Set a date as to when you will have attained your goal.

CHAPTER 4
DETERMINE YOUR PATH

ONCE YOU HAVE made a SMART goal, then you will need to set up an action plan. What will you create in the next thirty days? What do you need to do to get your goal? Write it out, and follow it on a daily basis. Keep track of your progress with some form of record keeping or journaling. You can look back and see just how much you have accomplished and be able to see the value of continuing on toward your goal. Many people who don't keep track of their progress get discouraged. You have to be able to show your results. Even if you simply start out with changing your normal daily attitude, keep track of every day that you do something different than the day before, such as repeating daily positive affirmations. When you look back at your progress, you will notice a considerable difference in your results just by having positive things to say to yourself on a daily basis.

There have been many times when I set a big goal, and I didn't know how I would attain it. Those are the times when it is crucial to always keep thinking about what it is you want. Keep your intention clear and focused on your desired end result. Intention is 100 percent commitment to whatever it is you want. When you are clear, the mechanism will appear.

At one point in my life, I had a used BMW 540i that I decided to trade in for a different vehicle. I didn't have a steady job at the time and was originally thinking of downsizing to a smaller used car (like a Honda Civic) because I was definitely in a scarcity mentality and didn't see how my financial status could change. It happened to be that the BMW had been in an accident before I bought it, and I was having a hard time getting a decent trade-in price. There was a Chrysler dealership that offered me the most for my trade. On the showroom floor, I saw a beautiful brand-new Crossfire. I had never seen that car on the street before. It looked fast and sleek, and it was way out of my price range. Instantly I knew it was the car for me. But how was I going to afford it?

This is where it pays to have friends with an abundance consciousness. I called a friend and told him how badly I wanted the new car. He asked me how many new clients it would take to be able to make the payment on it. (I was working as a personal trainer at a local gym to get by at the time.) I figured it

AFFIRMATION
I AM CLEAR ON WHAT IT IS I WANT.

would only take one new client signing on for training three days a week. I'll never forget the next phone call I got while I was waiting at the dealership. It was a referral from a friend who had set a physical goal and wanted to hire a personal trainer. He hired me over the phone. Promptly, I went and signed the paperwork for my new, beautiful car. I even got personalized plates that read "NTNTION" (standing for intention) to always be a reminder of this fact: when I am clear on what I want, a way will appear for me to get it.

It may seem scary along the way or you may begin to doubt yourself and feel you may have set a near-impossible goal. This is a perfectly normal emotion to experience. Clear intention is what will get you there and as long as you stay focused on your desired end result, the doubts will eventually disappear. This process requires a shift in your way of thinking, which doesn't always happen overnight. You have been thinking in particular patterns and with specific beliefs for years. It will take time and effort on your part to create new thought patterns and beliefs. You will have to force yourself and be regimented in creating your new habits. It will only take a short amount of time before you won't need to force yourself to think and act in new and positive ways. Be gentle on yourself and be forgiving if and when you happen to have a misstep and fall back into your old ways of thinking. You will eventually adjust to the new ideas, and the old ineffective thoughts will easily be pushed aside. The rewards that are awaiting you will allow you to pursue and attain ideas and objects you may now consider way out of reach. Nothing is out of reach when you just focus your intention and never let go.

At the end of the Wizard of Oz, Glenda the Good Witch reveals to Dorothy that she had the power within her to return home all along. Just the same, the power to achieve your dreams lies within you.

CHAPTER 5
EMOTIONS CREATE YOUR RESULTS

CHAPTER 5

EMOTIONS CREATE YOUR RESULTS

I am in control of and in tune with my emotions.

How are you feeling? Believe it or not, many people have a hard time answering that question. What makes you a human being? Your emotions do. Not only can we as individuals feel these emotions, we can also empathize with others and feel their emotions by proxy. Have you ever watched a movie where the main character overcame tremendous odds to win? You feel that win inside yourself as you watch. Now, have you ever watched a program where someone struggled with horrible circumstances? We see others struggling, and we feel that torment ourselves. Humans are the only animals who can empathize with another and feel his or her pain. This means our emotive functions are extremely fine tuned.

Many people think it is what they do that makes them who they are. They deny their feelings and shut themselves down emotionally, always pushing on to do more. Activity or productivity alone does not provide what you need emotionally, and to try to push aside feelings creates a void. Have you ever asked yourself why you don't get excited anymore like when you were a child? Or wish you could feel passionate about something—anything! Perhaps you have pushed aside your emotions and refused to allow yourself to feel for far too long. Some people think not feeling means not exposing themselves to disappointment. As though if you don't allow yourself to become very happy, then you also reduce the possibility of feeling very sad. You strive to maintain your emotions within a certain small range until it becomes habit. As a result, life becomes dull. Not only is it okay to show your emotions or feelings, it is necessary for your well-being to share them with other people.

I have a friend who, for much of his life, only allowed himself to feel angry or numb. It is very common in our society—for men in particular—to think that showing emotion is bad or indicative of a weak will. Pain often manifests through anger. When an individual shuts down emotionally in order not to feel any kind of pain, he will frequently use anger to power through whatever tasks he has to accomplish. The problem with shutting down is that you don't allow yourself to feel any pleasure either.

It is very common in our society to think that showing emotion is bad or indicative of a weak will.

My friend would use his anger to power through his day at work. That may be okay around the guys at work, but it didn't work for creating the intimate relationships he desired. So many boys are taught that "boys don't cry," and people will think you are acting like a sissy if you show your emotions.

Conversely, many women are raised with the idea that they should be sweet and not display any anger at all. When I was a child, I would get a spanking if I displayed my anger. (As if that didn't bring up more anger for me.) As a child, did you ever get told to "act normal" or "straighten up" when you were just displaying sheer joy by acting goofy or shrieking with delight? After being told time and time again to stop displaying our true emotions, as children we learn to hide how we feel.

AFFIRMATION
I AM IN CONTROL OF AND IN TUNE WITH MY EMOTIONS.

I'm sure most parents didn't mean any harm by their instruction as they were only raising us just as their parents had taught them. However, the effects can be debilitating as we lose the ability to be honest about how we feel with others and ourselves. As adults, we have a hard time meeting our emotional needs because we are so out of touch with how we are really feeling. It is virtually impossible to actually connect with other human beings when we ourselves are emotionally disconnected.

We discussed briefly in an earlier chapter how emotions create your results. Once you understand that concept, then it is obvious that if you refuse to allow yourself to experience emotion, you are creating self-limiting beliefs that can be very difficult to dislodge. You are constantly creating the story of you. What you feel and believe about yourself determines what is possible in your own mind, which then translates into reality. If you think crying or showing your love for someone is for sissies, then you are adding that idea to the story of you. You decide that you are not a sissy, so therefore you don't allow yourself to display the deep emotions you may have. This can result in those around you assuming you don't have any feelings at all. While you may feel deeply for someone, if you are unable to show it, then you risk losing what means the most to you.

Many people let their surroundings and outside circumstances determine how they feel. They live their lives in a reactionary mode. Have you ever felt sad and blamed it on the gloomy day? Or felt angry because you were stuck in traffic? Or happy because someone sent you a love letter? As most people do, I'm sure you feel justified in your thinking. However, none of those circumstances made you feel anything. You choose how you perceive your world, and thus you chose how to view each circumstance—just as you choose how you feel every minute of every day. And, you can change how you feel in an instant whenever you want to. There are some who don't mind being stuck in traffic because it gives them time to enjoy an audio book or think about the events of the day. Others love an overcast and rainy day that allows them to hear the raindrops falling and see nature renew itself. And just because you initially react one way does not mean you can't stop yourself and choose to feel completely different.

For example, imagine a mother who is very frustrated with her toddler for trying her patience for most of the day. Now imagine that same child gets in a locked room holding bare, electrical wires and starts to become interested in an open socket. Do you think that mother would forget all about her frustration with the child and do everything in her power to find a way into that room and save her child from harm? Of course she would. She would switch from frustration to love and care in an instant.

Nothing and no one around you can make you feel any particular emotion. But your environment can make it easier or harder. For instance, if you spend most of your time with people who are angry, jealous, and have a generally bad attitude, it may be harder to be upbeat and positive. In your workplace, wouldn't it be easier for you to be more productive and feel great about yourself if you have a boss that is encouraging and supportive instead of demeaning and faultfinding? Does your environment support you in being joyful, passionate, and excited about life? If you find yourself in a situation or surroundings that are not ideal or nurturing and don't feel you can remove yourself right away, you can still choose how you want to feel, and eventually your circumstances will change because of your emotional choices.

Does your environment support you in being joyful, passionate, and excited about life?

We are vibrational beings. All of our thoughts produce emotions with different vibrations. We are like radio transmitters and receivers. If you tune your car radio to FM 98.5, what will you hear come out of the speakers? You will hear whatever is being sent on that frequency. If you want to attract love, care, and happiness in your life, you must be loving, caring, and happy. You cannot get what you don't give. You must tune yourself into the frequency you want to receive.

AFFIRMATION
I AM IN CONTROL OF AND IN TUNE WITH MY EMOTIONS.

We each feel the vibration of those around us, and they feel ours. This is why you can meet someone and feel immediately at ease in their presence—they are on a similar vibration level. Now think about those people in your life whom you find hard to be around for any length of time. You are also feeling their vibration as vastly different from yours.

One of my colleagues has a family member who is extremely negative. My colleague jokingly refers to her as an "energy vampire." This is because she is so negative and needy that just talking with her feels as if he is having the life force drained out of him. It's exhausting, and though he loves her, he is unable to spend much time around her. One of the interesting aspects of ourselves as vibrational beings is that we are drawn to those of a higher vibration and repelled by those with a lower or more negative vibration. This is why we talk about motivational speakers or famous people as charismatic. Charisma is a result of a high-vibration level. They are the people everyone seems to want to know and be around. Spending time with those of a higher-vibration level raises your own, and spending time around those with a lower-vibration level lowers your own—which is why it is so important to choose wisely those individuals you spend time with.

You are an amazing and powerful being because you have the power of conscious choice. By using that power wisely, you will create an amazing life for yourself. Take control of your emotions. It's up to you to be happy, loving, genuine, and connected to the world. Enjoy!

CHAPTER 6
FREEDOM TO ACCEPT RESPONSIBILITY

CHAPTER 6

FREEDOM TO ACCEPT RESPONSIBILITY

I am living a life of true liberty.

We are born with the right to be free. And yet, so many people are left yearning and longing for freedom that they do not realize they are imprisoning themselves. Some may blame the way they were raised, the government, society, or plain bad luck for their lack of money and wealth. When, in fact, the only way to have true freedom is to accept full and total responsibility for your present circumstances. Now I do not mean you should feel badly about it or be overly critical of yourself. There is nothing to feel badly about. Taking responsibility means that you are choosing to take over the power to change your current status instead of staying in bondage to outside forces that govern your ability to have what you want.

CHAPTER 6
FREEDOM TO ACCEPT RESPONSIBILITY

When you get down to the determining factor for success in any area, it is the result of choices you have made in your life. You may not have chosen the specific destination, but the choices you made along the way have placed you exactly where you are today. We live in a blame society; everyone wants to blame someone else for virtually everything that happens to and around him. This blame trend is actually disintegrating empowerment in people's lives. No one is in control of someone else unless that controlled person allows it to happen. This means by blaming outside forces such as your boss, the economy, or your lack of education, you are choosing to give away your power and allow these other issues to control you. You can only accomplish total success when you are willing to accept responsibility for yourself.

THE FABLE OF THE BIRDS

There were once two baby birds named Charlie and Sam. These birds grew up together in upstate New York. They had a very happy childhood. They ate together and slept together. They learned to fly for the first time together. Then, their father taught them good places to hunt for worms. They were content and well fed. After a few months, the leaves began to change and a cool wind replaced the warm summer breeze. It was fall. One bright, fall day, their father was killed in a hunting accident when a cat leaped at him out of a nearby bush as he was fighting a worm. The brothers were devastated at their loss.

As winter closed in, the weather grew increasingly cold.

Charlie said, "Come on, Sam, we've got to travel south. We'll freeze if we stay here."

"No, thanks, I'll be fine," Sam replied. "I've lived here my whole life; there's no point moving somewhere now."

"But the winter's coming!"

AFFIRMATION
I AM LIVING A LIFE OF TRUE LIBERTY.

"No, I prefer staying here. I know all the hunting spots and hideouts here. I don't want to travel to unknown lands."

Charlie tried repeatedly to get Sam to change his mind, but it was no use. Finally, Charlie could wait no longer and flew south for the winter. Sam sat on the cold, icy branch of their tree and grumbled, "I can't fly south like Charlie because I'm still upset over my father's death. I can't be expected to undertake such a scary thing right now."

One week passed, and a winter storm blew in. Sam shivered and still grumbled, "Who can find food when the storm is so bad? It's not my fault that snow covers the ground. I'm doing the best I can, and that's all that I can do."

Another week passed, and Sam was weak and shivering, "I'm feeling ill. I can't fly south now; I'd never make it. Charlie was always stronger than me. He was special, and I'm just an average bird." The next morning, Sam lay frozen on the ground.

Charlie flew south, and Sam eventually froze to death because he preferred to stay within his comfort zone, even when circumstances changed. He refused to take responsibility for his own life.

Just like Sam, many people refuse to accept responsibility for their own lives. They go through life in denial or act like a victim. ("Why does this always happen to me?") By doing so, they voluntarily give up any chance for changing their own lives for the better. The first requirement of any kind of improvement in any area of your life is to accept the responsibility for what is.

I understand that you don't control the weather. You can't accept responsibility for the fact that it snows. You're not responsible for the snow or the rain, for that matter. But you are responsible for how you react to it. Do you get angry and upset when rain ruins your plans? Or do you just accept the fact it is out of your control and move on to something else?

Once you begin to accept responsibility for the current circumstances in your life, you will be able to release the past. We all know people who are stuck in one event, which may have happened years ago, and they can't move on. It may have been a traumatic divorce or the death of a loved one. That anger and hurt fester as the person continues to relive the experience. This may even be the case for you. Is there one horrible story you continue to tell others? If so, then that is the first hint you may be stuck in the past. That event no longer has any hold on you except what you give it. And by constantly rehashing it, you are refusing to accept responsibility for your emotions and let go of the hold it has on you. You must allow yourself the joy of the present and be unencumbered by past events. Otherwise, you cannot move forward.

A similar problem—and one that can be just as difficult to overcome—is living in the future. This is best illustrated by another story:

Many years ago, a man named Anthony lived in a small town. When Anthony turned thirty, he grew restless. He told his friends and family, "I am tired of this small town. I want to see new places. I will travel to the end of the world." They urged him to stay, but Anthony was adamant, so finally they let him go.

Anthony traveled for many years. He visited foreign countries where fruits were as exotic as plentiful; countries where herds of sheep were counted in thousands; places with mountains so high that their peaks reached above the clouds. But he was never satisfied. Anthony always grew restless after a few days, and looked longingly at the horizon. Soon, he found himself traveling again. The end of the world was much farther than he'd expected, but he was going to reach it.

He continued on his quest, and when he reached an ocean, he didn't even pause to look in awe at the huge mass of water. He immediately searched for a way to keep going. He found help from traders in a port and crossed the ocean.

AFFIRMATION
I AM LIVING A LIFE OF TRUE LIBERTY.

Anthony travelled for ten years, every day looking at the horizon, hoping he would finally reach the end of the world. And then, one sunny spring morning, he thought to himself, "This place looks familiar." He had reached his hometown. His friends and family had a huge celebration of his return. Anthony started telling them stories of his journey, and it was only then that he realized how many amazing things he'd seen and experienced. He marveled at how far he'd come. Yet he didn't even think of the wonder of it all while he was traveling; he was set too firmly on his target: the horizon. He never paused to smell the roses along the way. At that moment, he was enlightened, and he spent the rest of his time in this world enjoying every single day as it came.

Like Anthony, some people are permanently stuck in the future. They don't stop to realize the journey is the true destination. Think of your life one year ago. Who were you back then? What did you know? Realize how far you have come since then. How much you have learned, how much you have grown in character.

You can't change the past. You can't directly control the future.

This does not mean you should spend all your time in the present, like a car traveling with no direction. The past is useful because it contains valuable lessons, and the future is useful because you can plan where you're heading. But similarly to what Anthony experienced, getting stuck in the future will only result in you waking up one day, being seventy years old, and realizing you never took the chance to enjoy your life. It all sped by in a blur while you were on your way somewhere else.

You can't change the past. You can't directly control the future. Therefore, if you accept the responsibility for your own life, you must focus on the changes you can control in the present. Each and every decision you make today shapes your future, and only by making good choices now can that future be transformed into something wonderful.

CHAPTER 6
FREEDOM TO ACCEPT RESPONSIBILITY

I have often marveled at the number of rich and powerful people in the world who have come from poverty and who don't have the advantage of a great education—but still they overcame. How did they do it? I've come to the conclusion that they did it by being willing to take risks in their decisions. When they had the option to choose either the steady and known path, or the risky and uncertain path, they chose to be daring and prospered because of it.

You may think this doesn't apply to you and your situation, but it does. Even a small decision involving risk can greatly change your results. For example, many people are in some kind of service industry and are afraid to raise their rates or fees for fear of losing their existing clients.

When I was younger, I was a hairstylist. I had a great clientele and was consistently booked for a month in advance. I enjoyed giving quality, individual attention to my clients and didn't want to squeeze more people into my daily schedule. However, my bank account needed to have more money in it in order to do the things I wanted to. I knew there had to be a way to make more money and still give great service. Eventually, I realized that I was the only person who was responsible for giving myself a raise. Believe me, I was afraid to raise my prices. The concern of losing my clients weighed heavily on my mind. However, when I did give myself a raise, my results were amazing. I retained most of my clientele, and the time freed by the ones who didn't stay with me was quickly filled with new clients who were willing to pay more than my existing clientele. By taking responsibility for my financial well-being, I created more freedom with time and had more money to do the things I wanted to do.

Choosing involves risk, which is a good thing as it gives you the opportunity to change your life and improve your results far beyond what you can imagine today. And the best news is you can start immediately. Don't put it off. One year from now, you will look back at your progress and be astounded. But it will never happen if you don't take responsibility and exercise your freedom to choose.

CHAPTER 7
GIVERS GAIN

CHAPTER 7

GIVERS GAIN

I give of myself freely.

There are many ways to give. You can give your time, your money, your things and yourself. What does it mean to truly give? It means that you do not expect anything in return for what you are giving. In some way or at some level, you feel connected to everyone else and willing to share the good in your life with others. You do not withhold any of who you are and freely offer what you have to contribute. You come from a place of abundance; I'm enough, you're enough, there's enough for all.

This may seem counterintuitive in our world today as everyone seems so hung up on competing. Men have traditionally been raised to compete. In eons past, it was for food. Now, it is for money and power. While women have only been strongly in the workforce for the past three or four decades, we are now seeing the result of them being raised in that same, competitive environment.

CHAPTER 7
GIVERS GAIN

This competitive mindset often dominates the working world where we spend so much of our time and energy. It can be very difficult to grasp the idea of "givers gain" when you have been schooled to believe you should take care of yourself first. The idea of givers gain isn't about a trade-off; i.e., you give X to get Y. It is about a mindset and an approach to living that allow you to freely be yourself and open to others. This, in return, allows others to freely give back.

Sandy was raised with the idea you should always give back to others, no matter how little you have. When her children were in grade school, they had very little, but Sandy frequently engaged in small acts of giving whenever she could. She would bake a pie for the neighbor who had injured his leg and was laid up, or offer to babysit for an overworked career mom one night a week for free, and she would even save each year and offer to buy one needy child's school supplies. She kept a small cigar box which contained notes of what she did and when, along with the thank you notes from those she helped. This box reminded her of how often she was giving so she wouldn't forget and let too much time pass.

Your intention behind the gift is everything, and it can't be faked.

Eventually, as her children got older, Sandy got her realtor's license and started to sell real estate. She was told repeatedly it would take years to build her clientele, and it would be very difficult. But because she had done so many very small and wonderful acts of kindness over the years, people flocked to her and knew that she was trustworthy and sincere. She now makes more than $400,000 per year selling real estate.

It is important to note that Sandy did these things without an expectation of gain, but the gain happened. This is the core principle to understand when you decide you want to give. Your intention behind the gift is everything, and it can't be faked.

AFFIRMATION
I GIVE OF MYSELF FREELY.

Have you ever witnessed someone that gave a child an expensive toy as a gift and got upset because the child played rough and broke the toy? The person could only feel upset because he didn't truly give. He had a hidden expectation or condition of the gift being treated in a certain way. That was no gift at all. When you truly give, it does not matter what happens to the gift because you don't have any attachment to the outcome. You don't even expect a "thank you" because that's not why you gave. It just feels good inside when you give, and that is your only motivation for the action.

There is a law of the universe that is stated many different ways. Simply put, what you put out will come back to you. The law doesn't say from where you will receive. It will most often not be from where you gave but from another source entirely. Most people have heard of the concept that givers gain. They just haven't heard the entire saying, which is: Givers gain; unless they want to.

What are your motives behind giving? It's worth taking the time for a self-evaluation. If you already give, then why are you not getting the results you desire? Do you feel as if you give, give, give and never get anything in return? Look at your relationships. Are you giving a multitude of monetary gifts and not feeling loved or appreciated? Maybe, it's just quality time with you, which is the desired gift. Now don't get me wrong, most people appreciate gifts. They just don't want to feel as if they are being paid off in some way in lieu of the quality time. A relationship needs to be nurtured to grow. It is not uncommon for one partner to feel as if he is giving all of his time to provide a great life for his family, only to end up losing that family because what they really desired was time.

One of the main reasons people don't give is because of fear. Giving opens your heart to others through kindness. They may feel this leaves them exposed and vulnerable. The problem with this thinking is it usually stems from a situation that happened long ago. Perhaps one in which you felt hurt and rejected. When you live with this fear, you keep recreating the same outcome over and over again. If you expect to be rejected, you usually will be. Just the same, if you think you are going to be taken advantage of in a particular situation, you probably will be.

CHAPTER 7
GIVERS GAIN

One of my favorite fables is the one of the miser and his gold. This miser accumulated great wealth, yet he lived his life in poverty. He chose to bury his gold at the foot of a large tree. Every week, he would go and dig up the gold, run the wonderful wealth through his fingers, and then bury it once again. A thief who had noticed his pattern of activity waited until the miser had reburied the gold and then went and dug it up—making off with all the miser's money. When the miser came the next week to gloat over his treasures, he found nothing but the empty hole. He tore his hair and raised such an outcry that all the neighbors gathered around. He told them how he used to come and visit his gold and what a tragedy it was that it had been stolen.

"Did you ever take any of it out?" asked one of the neighbors.

The miser glared and said, "No, I could never do that."

"Then I have great news!" the neighbor motioned to the miser to come look at the hole. "See, you can still come look at the hole every week, and it will do exactly the same thing."

Wealth unused is the same as wealth never gained. We all are wealthy in different ways. It can be through our money, our time, our knowledge, or our experience. We each have something to offer and give back—whether that gift is financial or not. If we insist on keeping our wealth only for ourselves, it does no good.

A couple of years ago, my husband and I made a commitment to give to charity ten percent of whatever monies come into our household, no matter what. We believe we can make a difference, and it feels great! Sometimes, the amount has been less than $100 and may not seem like much, but if everyone gave even such a small amount, it would quickly add up. Since making the commitment to give, we have wanted for nothing. The money just keeps coming in, often from new and unexpected sources. I know it is, in no small way, because of the choice we made.

AFFIRMATION
I GIVE OF MYSELF FREELY.

Just like a boomerang curves in the air and comes back to you, whatever you throw out to the world will circle around and land back at your feet. If you smile at someone, in most cases they smile back; and if you're kind to people, they're usually kind in return. This also works in the other direction. If you complain to someone, they will share their complaints with you; if you get angry at someone, they will get angry with you. Some things come back right away, and some things take time. Nevertheless, you have a choice about what you want to come to you or what change you want to effect.

Another way to view this is to notice what happens when you drop a pebble in a pond. It ripples out over the water, effecting widespread change. The waves then hit the shore and come back to you in an even wider pattern. This is a great visual example of how the idea of "givers gain" works. You never know what the ripple effect will be of a small act of kindness. It could touch people you aren't even aware of and don't even know.

If you want more joy and happiness, bring happiness into someone else's life and watch happiness come back to you instantly. Need money? Give some away; give from your heart and connect with a feeling of abundance while doing so. If you give from the space of feeling guilty or think, "I really should give, even though I don't want to," you continue to create more guilt and feelings of being deprived. Bless your bills, and be thankful you can pay them. Spiritual leaders and financially successful people have been telling us this for eons, but we're afraid to believe it.

What you put out comes back. Yes, you will have bad days, so don't stress over the occasional bout with the blues or a dark mood. It's your overall generous attitude that will win in the end. But, if you gossip, complain, and share a lot of misery on a regular basis, you will amplify the presence of these things in your life and openly invite them to come back to you. In actuality, you will get more than what you share with the world.

The underlying principle is that happy people get happier, and unhappy, negative people get more and more unhappy. If you plant one seed, you don't just get one back; you get hundreds—maybe even thousands. I challenge you to find a way to give (to people you know and love as well as the stranger you meet on the street) every day. By doing this, you will discover an even more rewarding life.

CHAPTER 8
HIGHER POWER

CHAPTER 8

HIGHER POWER

I am connected to my higher power.

Most people believe that there is some kind of higher power. It doesn't matter if you call it God, Buddha, the Universe, the Divine, or just believe it is your higher self or superconscious at work. Your higher power, in whatever form it takes for you, is your source of intuition, inspiration, and brilliant ideas. We are spiritual beings having an earthly experience and have needs that reach beyond our physical existence. We all need time to nurture ourselves by enjoying nature, meditating, walking the dog, or whatever it is you do to connect with your source and renew your spirit.

Do you ever wish that you could ask for anything you want and get it? Actually, you can. We all have the capacity to focus our intentions and be granted what we want. You can think of it as your own personal genie. The genie's only job is to give us what we want and to say "yes" to our desires. Everything we have is directly related to what we have told our genie. Perhaps you wanted to work in a particular career. Your genie heard that request and set about making it happen. You recognized the opportunities and seized the moment when they appeared. Here's the story of a young friend named Joe who used this approach to get what he desired.

I am from Texas, and I got accepted into a great college in Memphis, Tennessee, four years ago. The summer before my freshman year, I stayed with my grandparents in Espanola, New Mexico. My granddad and my dad were both mechanics at one point, and they got me interested in working on cars. So I decided to take a part-time job at the local AutoZone because I thought it would be fun to be around car guys.

I really enjoyed the work and found out from my boss that the AutoZone corporate office was in Memphis. I started thinking, "Wouldn't it be cool to have a job there?" I studied finance and the next several summers stayed with my grandparents and worked at the AutoZone near their house. Come to find out, it is the top-grossing AutoZone store in the country. So I got to meet the regional manager on occasion as he frequented that store quite a bit. In the fall of my senior year, I decided to send an email to the AutoZone corporate office, even though they weren't hiring at the time. I explained when I would be graduating and told them about my wonderful experience working in the store in New Mexico for the last four summers. I mentioned that I'd met the regional manager and let them know I was very interested in working for them in any position that became available.

> *No matter what you want, your genie can really deliver if you let it!*

The human-resource manager thanked me and kept in email contact with me over the next few months. In April, before graduation, they asked me to come in and interview for an assistant-category manager position. The interview went great, and two weeks later, I got a call from human resources with a great job offer at the top of the pay scale for that position. Two days before I walked the stage to get my degree, I stepped into the office of my dream job. No matter what you want, your genie can really deliver if you let it!

AFFIRMATION
I AM CONNECTED TO MY HIGHER POWER.

Joe found out early if you let your genie work for you, you will get what you want—so why then are you not getting what you want? See if this sounds familiar: You say, "I want a new beach house in Maui." And your genie says okay and goes to work on how to make it happen. But then you have another thought that says, "I can't afford it." And your genie says okay to that, too, and stops working to make it happen. Your genie follows every instruction you give it, so if you say you want something and then follow with the thought that you can't afford it or you don't deserve it, then that will stop the genie in his tracks.

You may say, "I want to make 100,000 more dollars this year." Your genie says okay and once again sets off to make it happen. But then you have the thought, "I don't really deserve to make that much money," or, "I'm not qualified to go for that promotion." And your genie simply says okay and ceases to help you make more money. It is these conflicting messages that are keeping you from getting what you really want. You say you want certain things, but you have thoughts, feelings, and ideas working as counter intentions and therefore keeping yourself from ever moving forward.

So how do you know what messages you are really giving to your genie? Just take a look at your results, and you'll know instantly if you have been sending your genie mixed messages. Notice what that voice inside your head is saying. Many of us have negative dialogue that runs rampant through our minds and our lives. We expect wonderful things to happen or come to us, yet we spend the majority of our time focused on the negative. We talk about why we can't do something or have something and even go so far as to list the reasons why we will never get what we want. What kind of message is this sending to your genie?

Your genie can only say okay and go to work on solutions for you. Have you ever noticed how sometimes you have a problem that you've been working on for hours, and you eventually do something else—like go to sleep—and you wake up suddenly with a solution that just popped into your head? That was your genie at work. If you present where you want to go or what you want to attain, your genie will figure out the details.

CHAPTER 8
HIGHER POWER

You must become aware of how your random negative thoughts are interfering with your genie's ability to grant your desires. Once you become aware, you can then focus on changing those thoughts. Every time you notice you are giving your genie instructions that are negative, just remind yourself to concentrate on what you want instead of what you don't want. Eventually, you will train yourself to give clear instructions without wavering, and you'll be amazed at all the good things that come your way. Our thought patterns are habitual, and you choose if they are positive or negative (effective or ineffective). Once you become aware of changing your thoughts, you must also have faith and trust that what you say you want will indeed happen. Faith is the key ingredient to attracting abundance and staying connected to your source.

Those of us who are married or in relationships are doing this because we asked the person of our dreams to share his or her life with us. So, inherently, we all know we can realize our dreams merely by asking. And yet, after finding their mate and job, many people stop asking. As a result, they stop receiving. Their dreams vaporize before their eyes, and frustration sets in. Their progress is halted and happiness stunted.

So, inherently, we all know we can realize our dreams merely by asking.

Why do we stop asking? Mainly because we're afraid the person we're asking will say no. We are also afraid that we won't get what we want, and it's easier to not ask than be disappointed. Marcia Martin explains why such a notion is foolish: "What I point out to people is that it's silly to be afraid that you're not going to get what you want if you ask. Because you are already not getting what you want. They always laugh about that because they realize it's so true. Without asking, you already have failed, you already have nothing. What are you afraid of? Are you afraid of getting what you already have? It's ridiculous! Who cares if you don't get it when you ask for it because, before you ask for it, you don't have it anyway. So there's really nothing to be afraid of."

AFFIRMATION
I AM CONNECTED TO MY HIGHER POWER.

Another reason people don't ask for what they want is they are afraid they are unworthy of it. The solution is to make yourself feel worthy through action. I may want to get a raise at work, but I am not automatically entitled to one merely because I put in time and carry out my responsibilities; after all, that's what I am paid for. However, if I do more than I am supposed to and make myself a valuable member of the company, I feel worthy of a raise and can now ask for one with confidence. If I'm turned down, I can ask for advice on what else I can do to earn a raise in the future. So I have nothing to lose by asking. At the very least, I will gain some knowledge on how to better my chances in the future, as well as impress my superior with my ambition. At best, I will get what I want; so it's a no-lose situation.

It is important to learn from our children and even our pets. They live by the principle that there are no barriers at all to what they want; they don't hesitate to let you know what they want and when—sometimes very loudly! We need to do the same. It is essential to realize that we cannot reach our goals without the help of others. Therefore, we must ask. True, we may not get what we ask for, but we will never get what we don't ask for.

To get more out of life, we need to ask ourselves a series of questions. Questions such as, "What do I want that I am not asking for now? What is needed to get what I want? Who can help me get what I need? What are the obstacles I must overcome? What path of action should I take to overcome these obstacles? What are the worst and best outcomes of asking? What is most likely to happen? What am I waiting for?" Writing the answers to these questions will offer clues to some counter intentions that you may not be consciously aware of right now.

In the last chapter, we spoke about the idea of givers gain. In order to attract wealth and abundance into your life, you must be willing to cooperate with and help those who need your help. This does not mean that you should limit your generosity only to those who can also help you, but to anyone who needs it. Be generous and kind as this sets in motion relationships and networks that are predisposed to help you because you are worthy of them.

CHAPTER 8
HIGHER POWER

Need more help around the house from your spouse? Need more training to improve your job performance? Need your neighbor to stop blocking your driveway with his pickup truck? Need your doctor to explain in greater detail what your options are? Need help in doing your school report? Need to have your friend stop blabbing about the things you tell her in private? Accomplish your aims, achieve your wishes, and get what you want out of life by asking for it. Getting irritated and bottling up your desires only push you further away from what you really want.

In order to maximize your chances of success, here are some points to keep in mind as you are requesting help from others:

1. Explain your need and desire for help by making a request, not a demand.

2. Accept refusals graciously. Thank them for their consideration. Don't sulk. As the Russians say, "Ask a lot, but take what is offered." Show gratitude when help is given; show understanding when it's not.

3. Refuse to stoop to manipulation. Making someone feel guilty for refusing your request won't help you get what you want.

4. Accept responsibility to accomplish what you can without help first. Show some initiative.

5. Understand that asking for help will bring with it advice and suggestions that may be contrary to your own ideas. Accept them graciously and use what is helpful.

6. Operate under the idea of reciprocity: be willing to do for others anything you are asking someone to do for you.

AFFIRMATION
I AM CONNECTED TO MY HIGHER POWER.

7. Use prayer wisely and not as an excuse for doing nothing. God helps those who help themselves. Take action toward your dreams, and the path will become clear.

8. Be specific in your requests. Explain what you need instead of what someone is doing that doesn't help. Accentuate the positive, and you will receive more than you expect.

9. Realize no one can read your mind and cannot know the emotions you are experiencing or expectations you may have. Many married couples or close friends expect their mate or friend to be a mind reader. Unless you express your desires in a clear and understandable way, you should not be surprised if they guess wrong. Share your desires, and allow people close to you to come along on this wonderful journey with you.

10. Remain committed to your goals, and don't get discouraged when your requests for help are rebuffed. You will never lose unless you quit. Just keep on keeping on. The stakes are high, and your efforts will be rewarded—sometimes in ways that are not immediately obvious.

Asking for what you want doesn't mean you will get everything you ask for. But it does mean you will get much more than you ever thought possible. Imagine the tragedy of the many things that are lost simply because we are not asking for them.

I make a point of saying positive affirmations on a daily basis. On the instructions of one of my mentors, Bob Proctor, I state all wants as if I already have them and start them off with, "I am so happy and grateful now that ..." All of my wants are reality just making their way to me.

I encourage you to reach out, grab the fruit of life, and enjoy the many rewards that are yours just for the sake of asking.

CHAPTER 9
INTUITION

CHAPTER 9

INTUITION

I am trusting my intuition.

I'm sure you can think of a time in your life when you were faced with a decision and you instinctively knew what to do. Something inside told you the difference between what you could do and what you were meant to do. Many people interpret this as a hunch, a gut feeling, or an inkling. Call it what you will, this is your intuition.

The Latin meaning of intuition is "in to you." Makes sense, doesn't it? What a wonderful resource we each have at our fingertips, and it can be utilized without formal education or advanced skills. In order to start using it, all you need is to become aware of this amazing power within you.

Intuitive messages come in a range of ways, such as hearing actual words, visualizing a clear and distinct picture, dreaming, or as a deep, inner knowing or a quiet, subtle nudge. It's important that you become familiar with how your inner self communicates and how these messages will bring with them a sense of calm confidence. I began to pay serious attention and listen to my intuition during my training with Dr. Chérie Carter-Scott (www.drcherie.com). Developing and trusting your intuition are imperative to your success.

We have intuitive moments all the time, but we rarely pay attention. Why? Often, our negative dialogue steps in and says, "Who do you think you are to trust your intuition?" These thoughts convince us that we are imagining things and that it is silly to take action on a whim. But in fact, intuition is not a whim. It is feeling the energy of something or someone else. Our intuition is acting when we are correct about an inspired feeling without knowing why. It is something which happens instinctively from deep within us. Intuition is linked with intent; it is the bridge between the conscious, unconscious, and superconscious. Some people seem to have a more developed intuition than others. Many people trust "women's intuition" or "a mother's intuition," but this phenomenon is not limited to women. We all get inspired thoughts regarding the necessary or appropriate course of action.

Women may have a more developed sense of intuition simply because we have been conditioned to anticipate impending situations regarding our offspring or other persons in our care; and we instinctively act upon these instincts. Or maybe, just maybe, our intuition has developed more profoundly in some cases because we were told we have this gift, and therefore we see it as true about ourselves. It is part of our self-image.

One of the great things about intuition is that we never get an inspired thought that we are not capable of achieving. In situations such as this, the only question we need ask is, "Will this idea take me in the direction of my dreams?" And if the answer is yes, you must act on it immediately. Consider these two women who are business partners who could not be more different. They work fabulously well together as they complement one another's strengths and balance out the weaknesses. When one of them, Maggie, was asked how they even got together as business partners, she explained:

AFFIRMATION
I AM TRUSTING MY INTUITION.

Gina and I have been business partners for more than ten years, though when we met, finding a business partner was the last thing on our minds. Gina attended a continuing-education class at the local college one night when I was the guest speaker. After I spoke, I was chatting with the instructor, and Gina hung around and chatted with us, too. We hit it off immediately even though we are very different people. The one thing we absolutely have in common is our positive outlooks and sense of humor.

After that day, we kept running into each other in the strangest places. It really felt like divine intervention to both of us, and we seriously talked about our ideas for the future. We discovered that tremendous creativity flowed when we were together, and we both intuitively knew that this could be a really productive and profitable business partnership. In the last ten years, we've literally made millions. We've also laughed and cried and survived the tough times together because of our solid and unwavering belief that we are meant to be in business together. That initial spark of intuition has led us to great discovery about ourselves and what life can really be if you act on that instinct.

If you are not in the practice of consciously using your intuition, here is one technique I recommend in developing this faculty: first, you must recognize when your intuition has "spoken" to you and act upon it. When you initially try this, you may only realize your intuition at work after the fact. If you recognize you had an intuitive "hit," and it is too late to act upon it, that is okay. Either way, you must simply acknowledge and be grateful for the recognition that it is at work. The more you become aware, the more intuitive messages you will receive, and the more you will recognize them as they are occurring instead of later when you can no longer act on them.

There have been times when I have that little voice in my head say, "Pick up your cell phone," and then it rings. I have even argued with the voice, thinking I'll only be downstairs for a minute. Then I get a very important phone call I've been waiting for. I've heard, "Take this way home," instead of the regular route, and I end up avoiding a traffic jam or an accident. Whenever those things happen, I say a little thank you for having and listening to my intuition. The more positive attention I give to it, the more awareness I gain, and the more I recognize the messages.

CHAPTER 9
INTUITION

I now listen for and trust my intuition on everything from choosing which business deals I want to be involved in to carrying my phone with me when I walk upstairs in my home. You can enhance your awareness of your intuition as well. The following are some simple yet practical steps to help you develop your intuition. They will help you make decisions that inwardly feel right and reconnect with what you really care about. Finding your inner voice can give you the confidence and wisdom to face anything, and following it is the catalyst to living a full and rewarding life.

1. Learn to Quiet Your Mind

    Have you ever felt as if your mind races a hundred miles an hour, thinking and organizing all of the thoughts and activities of your day? I know I have, and we have become used to being constantly bombarded with messages and ideas. Our minds are often so filled with daily details that our intuitive voice gets drowned out. That's why it's important to carve out time to quiet your mind. This can be through meditation or simply spending quiet time alone. And this will allow you to hear your intuition beneath all that internal dialogue and chatter. Once you learn how to move away from distractions, you'll be better able to discern inner messages.

2. Tune In to the Energy Around You

    I'm sure you've had the experience of being around a negative person who can ruin your day. This is because you are allowing their negative energy to dominate your own. By tuning into the positive energy around you, you can improve your mood and perspective of events. This is critical. Positive energy feels invigorating, compassionate, and supportive; but negative energy is tiring, unkind, and critical. By intuiting these differences in friends and colleagues, you'll be clear about who is nurturing and who saps your strength. You cannot get intuitive information if you are always stressed and worn out. Many people find yoga very therapeutic for this reason. It is a quiet and serene way to get in touch with the energy that surrounds you as well as the intuitive energy within you.

AFFIRMATION
I AM TRUSTING MY INTUITION.

3. Your Dreams Can Help You

We dream several times per night. But dreams aren't captured by the intellect; you need intuition to grasp them. By paying attention to your dreams, you will engage your intuition. You may be surprised at the practical advice they offer, such as tips on romance and job stress. By initiating an internal dialogue with your dreams, you can receive ingenious solutions to your questions and problems. You can do this by posing a specific question and thinking about it as you fall asleep. You may ask, "Is the person I'm dating right for me?" The next morning, take some time before you get out of bed to remember your dreams. You can write them down so you don't lose any nuggets of understanding. Try this for five nights in a row, and see what you get. By allowing your subconscious mind to ponder the question in the dream state, it can give you answers and ideas you aren't aware of.

4. Be Open to This Process

It is essential to get past the ego that thinks you have everything figured out and be open to new possibilities and options. Your true path may not be the one you are currently working on, and for that idea to pop into your head can be a little disconcerting.

But still, YOU must understand that you are telling yourself something important. Even if that happens to be that you no longer want to follow your current career path, for example. It can be hard to listen to that idea when you've spent years getting educated in a particular field and have been working your way up. Ultimately, your own happiness is at stake, which is why IT professionals become high-school teachers and doctors open restaurants—they are following their intuition. When you ask yourself, "What's the next step?" you will instinctively know what you need to do. This is the time when you must begin to learn to trust yourself.

Intuition is not something you can force; the inspiration must simply be allowed to surface. Give it time to work toward your goals. Be open to the possibilities, and you will be rewarded with an instant knowing. Perhaps you'll have one of those "aha" moments—or two. Your intuition will enhance your personal growth and help you through the changes and transitions that life brings. Begin by putting it to work in small ways, and eventually your intuition (or sixth sense) will be as much a part of your life as your other five senses.

Some of you may find that your intuition speaks to you many times, and others not at all. That's okay. It can take time and commitment to develop this skill, but I guarantee you will create a huge difference in your life once you begin trusting this wonderful power already existing within you.

CHAPTER 10
JOYFUL LIVING

CHAPTER 10

JOYFUL LIVING

I am so happy and grateful for my life of joyful abundance.

Are you grateful for the life you have right now? You may not have everything you have ever wanted yet. And you may possibly not be all that happy about what you've created so far; and that's okay. As human beings, we are created to always want, be, and do more. If you hadn't ever experienced pain, you might not recognize the little, joyful times in life. Some people have been rejected or abandoned and have gone through more hurt than any human should have to. But, these same people can love and care more deeply and have greater compassion for others because of their painful experiences. Their experiences can be a source of great strength and power rather than an excuse to be miserable.

It is extremely valuable to be grateful for whatever it is you do have. When you are in a state of gratitude, your emotional and energetic vibration is raised to a higher frequency. You will attract what you think about the most. When you are grateful for what you have, you will attract more things to be grateful

CHAPTER 10
JOYFUL LIVING

for into your life, and it becomes easy to be joyous in the process. It is often constructive to take inventory on how many things you have to be grateful for. Make a game to see if you can come up with additional things over time. Notice how you feel while engaged in this action. Try it when you are waiting in the long line at the bank or the grocery store. Observe what effect your joyful state has on the people around you. You never know what difference you can make in someone's life just by sharing a simple smile.

Joyfulness is a state of mind. You choose joy just like you decide what outfit you will wear today. It's sad how many people don't allow themselves to feel joy and share it with others. By making joyfulness a top priority, you will have an enormous affect on the world around you. Some people who are close to you may not understand the changes you are making and might question you for your joyful attitude. They might even make fun of you. Sometimes, I feel as if people look at me like I'm little miss sunshine; no one can see me for what I have and feel inside. It's those times when you can share why you are joyful, and you can remind your friends, family, or co-workers

By making joyfulness a top priority, you will have an enormous affect on the world around you.

they have a choice, too. What difference can you make in their lives by truly caring and sharing your joyous spirit with them? Invite them to join you in feeling true joy about life instead of complaining about it.

Have you ever noticed your mood change because you were listening to someone else complaining? My husband was complaining to me about his irritation with a situation. He went on and on for a while. When he was done, we noticed I was now the one in a grumpy mood—all because he had just dumped his garbage onto me. It was so powerful to notice how being around someone who was complaining had such a huge effect on my mood. Both of us are now very aware and careful not to complain to each other. When we talk about our tough experiences, we try to find solutions or a different perspective instead of bringing each other down. And then we quickly move on. You must eliminate the habit of complaining. Nothing good can or will come of it.

AFFIRMATION
I AM SO HAPPY AND GRATEFUL FOR MY LIFE OF JOYFUL ABUNDANCE.

There are several different ways of finding and experiencing joy in your life. The first, and perhaps most important of those, is to know your purpose. Nothing will bring you joy more than knowing what you are meant to accomplish in your life. Not knowing can bring sadness, wondering, fear, and lack of fulfillment. Above all, discover what your unique purpose is here on this earth—then fulfill it. As you do, you will experience joy because you have found your true passion.

It is one thing to know your purpose, but then you need to live according to that purpose. This is a matter of priorities. Let your actions and schedule reflect your purpose. Don't react to circumstances and let them cause you to live without fulfilling that purpose. This will only cause frustration, anger, and bitterness—while living your purpose brings you deep satisfaction and joy. Rather than settling for the status quo and letting life drift by, strive toward the higher goals and purpose.

Almost everyone knows someone who is constantly, in some way, taking from those around him or her. In order to have real joy in your life, it is important to give more than you take. True joy lies in giving. While you can find a certain amount of happiness in accumulating, it will be a hollow gratification. Whether it is money, time, or just taking a moment to be kind, giving stays with you for a long time—buying stuff to make yourself feel better is fleeting and temporary.

Don't you just love to be around those who laugh frequently and heartily? I know I do. A good laugh can instantly improve your mood as well as the mood of all those around you. I recommend you laugh as much as possible. Most people are just too serious. We need to laugh a little—no, a lot! Learn to laugh daily, even if you have to learn to laugh in bad situations. Life is meant to be enjoyed, so it is good to allow yourself to laugh.

So how do you bring joy into your life if you're not in the mood for it? Can you just fake it? Can you have joy on demand? Many people have legitimate reasons for being somewhat despondent. When you're in that state of mind, how can you become joyful? You encounter people during the course of daily living who are naturally joyous and others that are seemingly much more somber and serious.

The opposite of joy is sadness, and these emotions are forces in our lives that have a very strong impact. If you saw the movie "Patch Adams," then you know how laughter can aid in healing. Joy is one of those underused tools, which by learning how to access it can really help us on a daily basis.

People often feel as if they are victims of their circumstances. If something in our daily life brings us joy, we are grateful for it. But is there something we can actually do to help us bring a joyous attitude that is not dependent upon circumstances?

In other words, joy is a completely natural state.

I've heard some wonder if joy is genetic. You do find people who are just naturally joyous, who have a kind of laid-back attitude that makes it enjoyable to be in their presence. And then there are others who may be very serious and are constantly bringing us down. We can learn a lot about this by observing children. Before society, parents, and community affect children, they can give us an idea of what our lives would be like if we were never abused, hurt, or disappointed. Children have natural cheer. They have a natural, enchanted air about them. Some people would call it innocence because children haven't yet tasted the pains of life, but you can also say that it does definitely reflect on a certain natural state we all have within us.

When does a child cease to be consistently cheerful? This happens when they taste disappointment or after they experience grief, loss, or letdown. In other words, joy is a completely natural state. Now, living in a world of so much grief and pain, when we see someone joyous, it's like a shock for us—an unusual experience. So a child's innocence serves them well because they

AFFIRMATION
I AM SO HAPPY AND GRATEFUL FOR MY LIFE OF JOYFUL ABUNDANCE.

haven't yet tasted what it means to live in a world of deception. Once they experience those disappointments, the joy bottles up to the point that it is difficult to access again.

> *That child, that cheer, that natural happiness and joy of childhood are locked within us.*

It's critical to see joy from this perspective, because if joy is an acquired state, something you develop at some point (later) in your life, then a very strong argument can be made that once you've lost a reason to be happy, there's no way of reconnecting.

However, if joy is a natural state of feeling a certain sense of belonging—a feeling within that you are important and you have value—then it's just a question of reclaiming that emotion, not creating something new. Joy is something that each of us has in our hearts. Even if you are the saddest person who hasn't smiled in years, you have a joy and gladness in your heart that may in some way be blocked or sealed away because you may not feel there's any reason to access it. But it's there, lying dormant in the depths of your being.

Many personal-development gurus and psychologists talk about your "inner child." The inner child has always been a reality. The concept is essentially the natural cheer, the natural spirituality, and the enchantment and magic of child life is maintained throughout our lives. However, once we mature into adults, our outlook on life hardens. By then, that child, that cheer, that natural happiness and joy of childhood are locked within us. Accessing and calling forth these qualities in your life will determine your happiness and joy.

You can look around at any situation and see when people are happy. For example, some are just happy with their job, and they are happy people. Usually, there are a few ingredients that contribute to their happiness. Ingredient number one is they feel needed and a vital part of the process.

They feel appreciated because they're doing their job; they don't feel neglected; they don't feel taken advantage of; they feel they belong; and their particular talents or strengths are being utilized and appreciated.

When you have that type of inner security, it leads to natural joy. Indeed, inner security is essentially the same as inner joy. Natural joy doesn't mean you get up to dance and celebrate at every moment, but it's just a certain feeling that you are wanted and needed. And when you have that, you have no reason to be sad.

CHAPTER 11
KNOWLEDGE

CHAPTER 11

KNOWLEDGE

I am continually gaining knowledge from my experiences.

To truly know something is different than knowing about it. Remember when you were young and memorized one plus one equals two? You knew about it as a concept. Then one day, you had a true knowing because you put it into use with two toys, or two apples, or two blocks. At that point, it became more than just a concept. You had an experience of what it meant. From this experience, you had a whole new understanding, which would stay with you for the rest of your life. That is real knowledge. It's not all the things you know about. It's having an experience resulting in a true knowing, which is then internalized as part of who you are.

As we continue to grow, we must constantly learn about ourselves. However, our society measures learning by retention of concepts taught to us. Learning is not measured by drawing forth the knowledge each one of us possesses and relying on ourselves for our answers. It is refreshing to know the personal-

CHAPTER 11
KNOWLEDGE

growth movement is on the rise and more people are interested in self-discovery. By learning more about yourself, you can communicate more effectively. Your communication will be at a level of truth and sharing of your essence rather than being superficial and phony. This is the only way to truly connect with another human being. You must first discover the "real" you—your wants, needs, and desires—before you could possibly share them with anyone else.

My husband started to delve into his path of self-discovery just before we started dating. He realized how he had shut down at an early age and had become apathetic toward others because he had been made fun of as a child. A severe car accident had left one side of his face paralyzed. He was tantalized by the other children at school, including his brother, which caused feelings of deep hurt. He had decided if he didn't care about anyone, then he could not be hurt again.

His business took off as he developed stronger business ties by caring about other people's wants and needs.

Through his self-discovery and gaining knowledge about himself, he began to open up and started connecting with other people. His business took off as he developed stronger business ties by caring about other people's wants and needs. He also started a healing process in his relationship with his brother, father, and other important people in his life. The more he learned, the more he shared with me. We developed a closeness that brought our relationship to a place neither one of us had ever imagined a relationship could get to. It can be so easy and wonderful to have emotional intimacy with your significant other.

Knowledge of self is a common goal essential for anyone desiring to achieve personal success. Many people are hung up on somebody else's idea of what it means to be successful, and they are unaware of what is truly important to them. This is completely normal. We all have important role models and influencers in our lives that may have basic values quite different from our own. If this is the case, it's important to recognize the discrepancy between what we have been taught and what we personally believe is truly important is due to a difference in perspective. If we spend our time and effort trying to meet somebody else's idea of success and ignore or belittle any conflicting messages from our own mind, then we will find ourselves frustrated, stressed, and unhappy.

So how do we go about realizing what's truly important to us? How do we recognize our weaknesses and learn not to hide behind them? How do we become balanced? How do we open that magical door directing us on the way to personal growth and success?

Knowing you are in complete and total control of your own destiny, no matter what happens or what others say, gives you the freedom to find your true self and determine who you will become. How many times a day do you hear someone say, "It's not my fault?" How many times have you said it? An incredibly destructive belief many people hold onto is the victim syndrome. This does not mean you have not experienced an unfortunate turn of events, but you must remember it is not the event that determines the outcome. It is your reaction to the event and your acceptance of responsibility. If you decide to face each difficulty with the attitude of "poor me," then that is exactly what you will get: a poor life.

Not all of us examine our belief systems as young adults. In fact, we can hold off and live blissfully unaware there is anything amiss—until there is a catalyst jolting us into questioning who we are and what we really believe. This could be a general dissatisfaction with the life we have, especially if it falls short of our expectations. Or it may be something more traumatic, like divorce or the loss of a loved one. A catalyst can be nearly anything calling into question what we have known to be true most of our lives.

One of the wonderful things about being human is this fact: we all have the ability to change ourselves. Many people have experienced the glory of a transformational epiphany that has redirected their entire lives. They stepped

CHAPTER 11
KNOWLEDGE

back and recognized they too had a choice—the kind of power each one of us possesses—then set out to harness that power for themselves. You can have this same transformation in your own life.

There are many ways and paths on your own personal journey of self-discovery and transformation. I highly recommend going through a personal growth seminar (such as PSI Seminars: www.psiseminars.com or The MMS Institute: www.themms.com) produced by a professional seminar company. I also recommend meditation, reading thought-stimulating books, and/or hiring a personal coach. No matter what road you take to discovery, always remember it takes action on your part to make the differences you are seeking.

Knowledge is nothing without action. Incorporate what you learn into your daily life. You may struggle with this at first. You might even have to force yourself to start making some changes. Ask a close friend for support if you need to. And always remember and stay focused on what it is you want to create. As you continue making these changes, you will notice it becomes easier. You will have developed habits that serve you in getting what you want. You won't have to put so much mental energy into doing it anymore. It will just become automatic for you to make choices that will serve you.

Stay focused on what it is you want to create. As you continue making these changes, you will notice it becomes easier.

I'm not saying you won't continue to have challenges in your life. There will always be situations that come up for you that will serve as opportunities for growth. Life is about constant learning. Do you remember a time when $100 seemed like a lot of money to you, and that was all you thought you needed? You wouldn't have much money now if you never set your sights higher than $100. Once you've reached a goal, you will discover another want or need and have an opportunity to strive to achieve it. You can have fun with this process and challenge yourself to get what you want in a shorter time frame, or you

AFFIRMATION
I AM CONTINUALLY GAINING KNOWLEDGE FROM MY EXPERIENCES.

can just set larger goals. If you have what you need as far as money goes, then why not set a relationship, fitness, or spiritual goal? Strive for balance in your life. What good is a lot of money without someone to share it with? Or without having your health?

Having the attitude that learning is fun will serve you in the process of gaining knowledge about yourself. Keep in mind you are gaining this knowledge for the purpose of knowing and getting what you want out of life. Keep it light, and don't take yourself so seriously. When you have a profound moment of self-discovery about a part of you that you are not proud of, you must laugh at yourself instead of being hard on yourself. Learning to love all of you—including your dark side—is invaluable to unlocking your fullest potential. You'll be more apt to continue on this path if you are kind to yourself in the process. Janet's story illustrates this idea.

I was always a chunky kid and suffered a great deal from the teasing of others when I was young. My weight yo-yoed more than I cared to admit in my early adult years. When my first marriage dissolved, I made a decision to lose it for good. And I did. Unfortunately, I was a basket case! I'd cry at the drop of a hat and then get paranoid that someone didn't like me for some reason. It wasn't until I went through a personal development seminar that I realized that I'd lost the weight on the outside but was still carrying around the hurt from my childhood experiences. I learned to release that hurt and not take things so seriously. If someone liked me, fine; if not, that's okay, too.

I really feel that the reason I was overweight to begin with was that I carried the burden of anything and everything around with me, and the weight was just a physical manifestation of that fact. Humor was key for me in overcoming my need to be perfect. I learned to laugh not only at myself, but also at life and those strange and unnerving circumstances that happen. No one was harder on me than me. And I finally let that go and allowed joy and excitement back in. No one ever lost anything by learning more about who they are and what makes them tick.

CHAPTER 12
LESSONS

CHAPTER 12

LESSONS

I am so happy and grateful that I acknowledge and learn from my lessons.

Everyone has had times in his life where he hurt or felt shame, anger, or even abandonment. Perhaps something happened that you had no control over, or perhaps it was a decision you made that precipitated the event. We all have done things we are not proud of, and, especially when we are young, making mistakes is how we learn. Most of the time, we feel these negative emotions because of what our parents or someone else said to us about what happened.

It is important to know that nothing you've ever done or that has happened to you was wrong in the true sense of the word. Yes, bad things do happen. And many children don't deserve to have experienced some of the terrible things that happen to them. But these things do and did happen in childhood. Many people later in life still struggle with events and circumstances from their childhood. While the past cannot be changed, we do have a choice in what it means in our lives today. This includes choosing to view the event from a

CHAPTER 12
LESSONS

different perspective and using the lessons from our life to help ourselves and others. Unpleasant events are never welcome, but once they happen, they can allow you to have a deep understanding and compassion for those who have experienced something similar.

No matter what has happened in your past, there is much to learn from what you have gone through. Instead of using our hurts as an excuse not to move forward in our lives, we can use these experiences to propel us upward and onward toward our goals. I challenge you to take anything that has happened to you and find out what lesson is there for you to learn. What can you use from that experience to make you a more successful human being?

As I mentioned earlier, I was not raised with monetary wealth. In fact, throughout my youth, I was just above the poverty level. It affected me emotionally, and I felt less overall self-worth than other people I knew. I always felt as if I was being compared to everyone else and was found lacking.

When I turned sixteen, I wanted out of the strict religion my parents had raised me in, and because of that choice, I had to move out of their house. I left with just my clothes in plastic garbage bags. I didn't even have a job. Needless to say, I felt hurt, abandoned, and just plain down and out—completely rejected and unwanted. During the first few months of leaving home, I lived with friends for a week or a few at a time. Things could have gone pretty badly. I could have ended up on the streets doing drugs or who knows what else, but I didn't. Instead, I chose to move to a different state to live with my aunt and uncle and finish high school.

That way, other people wouldn't have high expectations as I didn't have high expectations of myself.

There are so many things I learned from my experience. But for years, I used the story to get sympathy and have people feel sorry for me. That way, other people wouldn't have high expectations as I didn't have high expectations

AFFIRMATION
I AM SO HAPPY AND GRATEFUL THAT I ACKNOWLEDGE
AND LEARN FROM MY LESSONS.

of myself. I was a very angry and sad person who wouldn't allow anyone to get close. I had to be in control all the time, and yet I felt completely out of control. In short, I was miserable.

Now, after looking back on all the events that transpired, I can see the lessons that were there for me to learn. I have learned that I always had support around me when I needed it. I also learned I have a huge reservoir of strength and courage within me and not only can I survive through adversity, I can and will thrive. I will make it through anything and come out on top.

The result for some people who are still carrying pain is they have very negative beliefs about themselves. They may not feel they have any choice other than to relive those negative emotions repeatedly—but they do. By choosing and committing to a new awareness and mindset, you will eventually change your belief about yourself.

It is interesting how many people I talk to who think these ingrained beliefs must have come from a big, traumatic experience when actually the opposite is true. Most develop their beliefs about what they can or cannot accomplish from even the smallest of events. This is because as children, these events take on a larger-than-life reality for us. Have you ever revisited a home that you lived in as a child? Were you surprised at how small it now seems when you remembered it much larger? Now think about an incident that may have happened on the playground or in the classroom when you were embarrassed or made to feel less than intelligent. While in reality the event may have been quite minor, to you it was incredibly traumatic.

Words spoken by a parent or loved one can affect your belief about your potential and your ability to change for the rest of your life—if you allow that to happen. You may have family or friends that constantly tell you to quit dreaming and focus on reality. You have to decide if you will let them limit your life.

CHAPTER 12
LESSONS

Each one of us must remember it is not what we are born with or without that determines who we will become. By the same token, you cannot blame others for your success or failure as this is the road to irresponsibility and helplessness. You can only change yourself and the way you relate to other people. This is the path to true happiness and success.

Knowing you are in complete and total control of your own destiny, no matter what happens or what others say, gives you the freedom to find your true self and determine who you will become. As mentioned in the last chapter, viewing yourself as a victim of life rather than a participant weakens your resolve, and it is very easy to feel trapped and remain the victim for your whole life.

Part of your internal dialogue may be that you are not very smart, not interested in the right things, or the things you want are out of reach. There is an old saying, "Misery loves company," and so it makes sense that many of the people in your family or peer group may have this same internal dialogue. Unfortunately, when one person in a particular group strives to achieve something beyond what the group is used to, the reaction is negative rather than positive. We all live in a certain comfort zone, and if one of the individuals within that zone steps up to a new level, the others will inevitably try to pull him back. This is an interesting dichotomy unique to humans. We are social creatures and want to belong to a group. However, if that group is holding you back, then you must go forward, even if it means severing some of those connections.

When you look back on your life, I'm sure you can find many valuable lessons you have learned. Forgive yourself for wherever you feel you may have fallen short. Be assured, you are on a path leading to greatness and know anyone may stumble now and then. The harder the obstacles were for you to overcome, the more you have to offer other people. Your strength, perseverance, and values are an inspiration to others if you allow them to be. You can support those you care about through their tough times by knowing they can make it through just as you have. Give yourself credit where credit is due. Acknowledge how truly wonderful you are and share your greatness with all whom you meet.

CHAPTER 13
BEING MAGNETIC = IN ALIGNMENT

CHAPTER 13

BEING MAGNETIC = IN ALIGNMENT

I am so happy and grateful I am attracting all I need to fulfill my purpose.

Do you know what your main purpose is in life? It's important to be clear on what your definite, main purpose is, otherwise, you risk floundering about with no real direction. Without purpose, it is impossible to know what goals are right for you or which actions will be the right ones to bring about your goals. Each of us has a reason for being on this planet. Every person is special and unique, and there will never be another individual exactly like you. There is a way that only you can give to this world. And, it is up to you to discover what that way is and say "yes" to it. There is a saying that goes, "God never asks about our ability or inability, only about our availability." Are you willing to make yourself available to your purpose? If your answer is "yes," then search inside your heart and mind for your answer. Listen to what your inner voice tells you. Discover your unique gift to the world.

CHAPTER 13
BEING MAGNETIC = IN ALIGNMENT

Once you have allowed yourself to put your purpose into words, you then have a reference point to check your goals and wants against. Does your goal serve your purpose or does it draw you away from it? Only you really know. When your goal is serving your definite purpose, you are in alignment. A magnet will attract when it is in alignment at an atomic level. You too are a magnet—you must be in alignment to attract what you want. If your goals are not in alignment with your purpose, you will repel the very thing you want to attract.

It's not just your goals that must be in alignment. Your thoughts must be as well. My husband and I have a friend, Sam, who is a real-estate agent. When the market shifted, he found himself struggling to make ends meet. Sam would call and complain about how bad his situation was, his clients, the houses he was showing, and just about everything he could think to complain about. One day, my husband shared with Sam how a shift in his mindset would benefit him immensely. He reminded Sam to stay focused on his goal and not let the market dictate what he wanted to create. By doing this, he would, at the very least, have a better mental attitude and be pleasant to be around; and at best, he would have more business than he could handle. A month or two later, Sam called and was so excited to share about his recent increase in business and accelerated closings. He attributed this sudden improvement to the changes he made by focusing his thoughts on what he wanted instead of what he didn't want. He was so grateful for having my husband as a friend who supported him by setting him on the right track. Sam got these amazing results because the shift in his thinking was now in alignment with what he wanted.

Focus on why and how you can, and you will attract solutions to you.

Whatever you are thinking about most is what you will attract into your life. If you think about how hard it is to get what you want and how miserable you are, you will attract more things to be miserable about, and it will be hard to achieve your desired results. When you are focused on positive ideas,

AFFIRMATION
I AM SO HAPPY AND GRATEFUL I AM ATTRACTING
ALL I NEED TO FULFILL MY PURPOSE.

you will attract more things to be happy about and grateful for. Directing your attention to being grateful, loving, and passionate will magnetize you to attract more to be grateful, loving, and passionate about. Focus on why and how you can, and you will attract solutions to you.

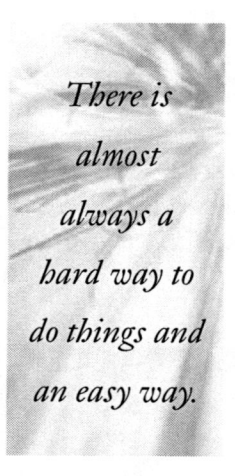

> *There is almost always a hard way to do things and an easy way.*

When your thoughts are aligned with your purpose and goals, you will not have to work hard at achieving what you want. You will have leverage to easily create what you want. There is almost always a hard way to do things and an easy way. If you are already working hard toward your goals, working harder won't get you the desired result. Imagine, on the side of the road, a car with a flat tire. In order to change the tire and put a spare on, the car must be lifted up. It would be possible to get a bunch of people to hold the car up, but that would be completely impractical and would require a lot of unnecessary effort. The easiest way to lift the car up is with a jack. And you could do that all by yourself.

Purpose is the why—why you do what you're doing. It is the basic engine driving your life. As you set about discovering what your purpose is, it is important to understand it is not something you seek or something that comes from outside you. It is a part of who you are and can only come from within. You cannot ask others. It is useless to ask friends or family what they think your purpose might be. The best they can offer is their view of you based on their own beliefs. Just as you can never imitate someone else's passion, others cannot guess what your passion will be, and they may even discourage you from chasing your dream because of their own fears or assumptions. As you look within yourself at your talents and gifts, you must set aside any negative thoughts or practical rationales. These are just fear in disguise, and you cannot allow them to inhibit your future.

CHAPTER 13
BEING MAGNETIC = IN ALIGNMENT

Defining your purpose can lead to startling discoveries. Some professionals even abandon their training in one area to take up their true purpose, which lies elsewhere. There are literally millions of people just like you who may be frustrated and bored with their profession but feel trapped. They feel like one spoke on an ever-turning wheel—doing their duty to provide while sacrificing their true purpose and passion. It is all about choice. Once you find your purpose, you will find a way to fulfill it—so you can't let fear convince you otherwise.

But what if you've tried before and failed? Every single person you see or meet has failed at some point in his or her life. This includes you, me, Oprah Winfrey, Bill Gates—everyone. It is important to understand that when we fail, it's not our intentions at fault. We failed because our guidance system was off. We are not in alignment with our purpose, so it just didn't work. It is very tempting in this situation to think back and look at the things we might have done differently. This is like running the "what-ifs" in reverse. What if I'd said this or done that? This replay of the past is a complete waste as the past cannot be changed. But if you constantly live in a mindset of "shoulda, coulda, woulda," then it will adversely affect your future.

Another common mistake is people get so completely carried away with the details of plotting the goals and steps within their purpose they never progress beyond the planning stage. You will see this frequently. They talk about their plan, and it sounds great; but they never put it into action because they are always trying to work out one more detail, one more unknown. They get so caught up in planning, charting, and graphing their future they never actually do anything. This is nothing more than a way to hide from their fear. Your plan doesn't have to be perfect. Get the basic ideas in place and get moving.

You must not lose sight of the fact you are beginning an incredible journey. It is not just about accomplishing great goals; it is also about enjoying your life as you go. You will meet wonderful people as you travel your unique path that will add untold joy to your life. Take the time to appreciate those friendships and relationships adding to your quality of life.

AFFIRMATION
I AM SO HAPPY AND GRATEFUL I AM ATTRACTING
ALL I NEED TO FULFILL MY PURPOSE.

You must create the mindset that you can and will have what you want and you will get it easily. This does not mean you won't have to work for it. It just simply means you don't have to run yourself ragged to meet the goal, and you can have so much more fun by being joyful along your path to success. Work diligently at it every day. You will feel energized instead of run-down because you know you are in alignment with your purpose. All you are thinking and doing is bringing yourself closer to your dreams. Become a magnet for all your wants and desires—and watch your dreams become reality.

CHAPTER 14
NOW

CHAPTER 14

NOW

I am taking advantage of every opportunity to fulfill my purpose now.

Have you been waiting for the perfect time to have children, start your own business, live where you really want to live, etc? There is no perfect time, and it is always the perfect time. The universe is just waiting for you to decide when you want it. Once you've made the choice and taken an action step, the universe will get in alignment with what you want.

The only time we ever have is right now. Have you ever had someone close to you die without warning, and you wished you had expressed how much you loved them or how much they meant to you before it happened? People live and act like they are going to live forever. However, the truth is, we are all going to die someday. And unless we have a terminal illness, we usually have no idea when it is going to happen. Intellectually, we know we will die, but hardly anyone lives life that way. We put things off all the time. We say,

CHAPTER 14
NOW

"I'll tell her I love her tomorrow; I'll ask for that raise next week; I'll take my dream vacation sometime when I can afford it." How long do you think you have? Not as long as you may think.

Even when we think we are floating along on the accepted path of life, we have no idea what the future holds. Jean is now in her forties and tells about her experience with the idea of "now."

I got pregnant in high school and had three children before I was twenty-three. At the time, I had numerous people tell me I had ruined my life, and there were times I thought maybe they were right. All my friends left for college, and there I was with a bunch of babies to raise. It was a struggle, and I wondered if things would have been better had I chosen a different path and put off having my children until I was closer to thirty. I did eventually get my degree, now I also have an MBA and started my own business, which is very successful. About the time I turned thirty, I went through sudden and immediate menopause. There was no warning, and nothing they could do to stop it. It became clear to me that had I waited to have children and gone to college first and started a career as many of my friends did, I'd never have had the opportunity to have any of my own children at all. Now, they are all grown and have left home to start wonderful lives on their own, and I am thankful everyday that I got to have them. There is no such thing as the perfect time. Now is great—and in truth, it's really all we have.

Many people are unhappy because they just cannot live in the present. Most of the time, their minds are hovering either in the thoughts involving past failures and unhappiness, or they are thinking about the future and feeling some sort of fear of the unknown. Scientists have stated that 90 percent of our lifetime is spent thinking about either the past or worrying about the future.

We all focus on our health and seem very concerned with adding days to our lives. Are you forgetting to add life to your days? If so, you are not alone. This is a problem many of us have, and it is the reason we should all try to make a conscious effort to live in the present moment.

AFFIRMATION
I AM TAKING ADVANTAGE OF EVERY OPPORTUNITY
TO FULFILL MY PURPOSE NOW.

When we are living in the moment, we are totally immersed in and focused on what we are doing. While there are times we need to evaluate the past or plan for the future, we should be aware that obsessing in either of these areas will not help us meet our goals effectively.

It is easier to live in the present than you might think, and it begins with you being conscious of your thoughts. Make a mental note whenever you find yourself focusing on something negative. Are there certain thoughts that come up more frequently? Often, negative feelings are based on something from the past or something you may fear in the future.

Write the negative thoughts that occur most often in a notebook, and then make a list of positive thoughts to replace them with. As you train yourself to replace these negative ideas with more positive ones, you can move on to tackling more concerns. You can also use this technique to get to the root of the real problem. Are you emotionally attached to something in the past that you can't do anything about and can't change? Is this bringing up negative thoughts that aren't really valid today? Remember to focus on the present and what you can affect. Now, see if you can identify the problems that are fear based. Are you afraid something will or won't happen in the future? Are you letting fear inhibit your life and affect your decisions? Fear can be one of the hardest things to let go of. We all experience fear and concerns over the future, but when those negatively affects our now, then we have to identify those thoughts and release the fear.

This process is about awareness—nothing more, nothing less. You need to be aware of your thoughts, not just let them run wildly through your mind. This is the first step to living in the present moment. Even if you are only in the moment for a few minutes a day, it's better than not at all. So now, when these thoughts come into your head, stop yourself from letting them bother you; let them go. Doing this will be easier because you are now aware of these thoughts and know what you can and can't control. Now you can replace those thoughts with everything you are grateful for right now (the present

CHAPTER 14
NOW

moment). Just be at peace with this moment and with yourself. Now, think about this: the only moment in which we can truly be happy is the present moment. The only moment we have control of is the present moment. So let go of the negative thoughts and be happy now.

Indecision is a great killer of goals because it takes away your need to act now. It causes you to lose momentum and lose your enthusiasm and excitement. Time slips away while you wait for the perfect moment. Once you know what you want, you must take action. Maybe you have set a huge goal, and you don't know how to go about it. The only way you'll ever get it is if you start working toward it immediately rather than just waiting. Take an action step right away. Your first action step can be as simple as writing out an affirmation. Have it end with a date by which you will have achieved your goal. Begin all your affirmations with the words "I am." State your affirmation as if you already possess whatever it is you want. Close your eyes and picture yourself as already having what you desire. Allow yourself to feel happy and grateful because you know you already have it in your mind. Know you have all you need inside of you to make your goal a reality. Your affirmations may look something like this:

Indecision is a great killer of goals because it takes away your need to act now.

- I am so happy and grateful that I am a successful business person and have increased my sales two-fold this year.

- I am so happy and grateful that I am a mother of a beautiful baby that my husband and I love very much.

- I am so happy and grateful that I am a newlywed and now have a wonderful life with the girl of my dreams.

- I am so happy and grateful now that I have a passive, residual income of $107,000 a month.

AFFIRMATION
I AM TAKING ADVANTAGE OF EVERY OPPORTUNITY TO FULFILL MY PURPOSE NOW.

ONCE YOU HAVE come up with your affirmation and allowed yourself to feel in possession of your goal, then your consciousness will start to take over. You will attract to you all the things you need to succeed.

When I decided I wanted to be in a committed relationship again after I had been divorced, I set a new relationship as a goal. My affirmation sounded like this, "I am so happy and grateful now that I have a healthy, fun, spontaneous, number-ten relationship with the man of my dreams," and the kicker, "within ninety days." I surely felt the butterflies come up in my stomach after saying that out loud for the first time. I also knew what I wanted and was not going to wait. I memorized and kept repeating my affirmation every day. Within two months, I was dating Gideon. I got exactly what I wanted. We were married about a year later. I am constantly grateful for setting such a specific relationship goal as it allowed me to have a fun and exciting marriage based on love and appreciation.

I don't know if I ever would have gotten married again had I not been clear on what I wanted and taken action to achieve it. When you are staring a big goal in the face, it's important to keep things in perspective.

> Question: how do you eat an elephant?

> Answer: one bite at a time.

ANYTHING CAN BE accomplished. You wouldn't have the desire for something if you did not also possess the power to make it a reality. Just start the forward momentum by taking action now. The excitement and energy you create will pull you forward and attract all you need. If you start to doubt yourself, go back to your affirmations and visualization. Always visualize the perfect end result. Instead of thinking why you can't, ask yourself how you can. Remind yourself that yes you can have it and you deserve to have it.

CHAPTER 15
OPPORTUNITY

CHAPTER 15

OPPORTUNITY

I am so happy and grateful to recognize and act on great opportunity.

Have you ever passed up an opportunity only to regret your decision later? Think back to why you didn't take advantage of the idea when it came along. I'm sure there are some people who wish they had invested in Microsoft when stock first became available. At least some of those people thought they could not afford to make the investment at the time. If they only had known then what they know now, they would have found the money somehow, knowing the return they would have made on the investment.

Once, I heard a story that Bob Hope used to tell. He was one of the first people Walt Disney approached about an amusement park that Walt wanted to build. Bob Hope said he dismissed the idea, thinking Walt was misguided if he thought people would drive out to Anaheim just to go to an amusement park. That park, of course, became Disneyland and helped create the Disney empire. Needless to say, Bob Hope regretted passing that one up!

CHAPTER 15
OPPORTUNITY

You've heard that hindsight is 20/20, and it's easy to point out what you should have done after the fact. But how do you have that kind of vision when the opportunity is in front of you? How are you able to discern the good choices from the bad? The only way to choose wisely is to listen to your intuition. As you tune into your intuition, you'll recognize that voice in your head telling you when to seize an opportunity. When you hear it, you must find a way to follow your intuition. You will also recognize when it's just fear standing in your way again.

ALL THE OPPORTUNITIES you need to become wealthy already exist around you. They have just been blocked by your current beliefs. If you have been telling yourself for years you can't afford nice things, you don't deserve to have what you want, and you aren't worthy, then of course you won't be able to recognize the opportunities in front of you. You will be blind to them because they do not exist for you in your consciousness. "Those things are for the smart, fortunate, or privileged people—but not for me," is what you say to yourself. Saying your affirmations on a daily basis is a great defense against this way of thinking. The negative things you have been telling yourself are lies. However, you've said those things to yourself for so long that they feel like the truth. It might feel as if you are telling yourself a lie when you start to say your affirmations. Your mind is quite powerful. When you tell yourself something long enough, you will eventually believe it. The choice is up to you. What do you want to believe?

The negative things you have been telling yourself are lies.

You've probably heard the saying, "every cloud has a silver lining." It's true, if you are looking for it. Think of a time when you were at a low point in your life. I felt down and out when I went through my divorce. I was embarrassed because I couldn't make my marriage work. I had just started my own business and wasn't bringing in a steady income. I couldn't afford to live on my own and had to rent a room from a friend who was ten years younger than myself. There I was at thirty-one years old, starting over again. I felt like such a failure. Of course, I wallowed in my misery for a little while. Then my personal coach asked me, "Didn't you want to get divorced? Weren't you miserable? Wasn't this your choice?" I had to agree with her.

AFFIRMATION
I AM SO HAPPY AND GRATEFUL TO RECOGNIZE AND ACT ON GREAT OPPORTUNITY.

I had made my choices and now had to deal with them. There was a great opportunity in front of me to start over. I could now create the life I wanted; there was nothing holding me back. I chose from that point forward to be happy and go for what I wanted. That year, I accumulated the most money I had ever made, I found the love of my life, and I started traveling all around the world. I took the opportunity to get passionate about what I wanted in life and started creating it. From one of the lowest points in my life, I was able to skyrocket up into the life I had always wanted. Whatever point you are at in your life, you can use it to propel you forward toward your dreams—as long as you are looking for the opportunities that are right in front of you.

You may be thinking that I'm crazy and that your life isn't rife with those opportunities that I'm talking about. I once thought that way too, but the truth is the opportunities are there—you just haven't learned to see them or recognize the fact they are there. There are several ways to jump-start your ability to find opportunities. They include:

Seek out and develop relationships with highly creative people.

CREATIVE PEOPLE HAVE honed their ability to see opportunity to a high level. They see opportunities everywhere, and their insight will rub off on you. The best way to learn to see a world of possibilities is to choose to be around people who spend most of their time actively creating things. These people may create art, literature, businesses, graphics, websites, ideas, music, markets, products, or anything else constructive. Find ways to spend your days and nights talking about creative ideas and thinking about possibilities. You can do this through finding a mastermind group, hiring a life coach, or finding like-minded, creative people online through social networking sites. Your opportunity to meet other creative people and share ideas is greater than ever before in human history. No matter where you are, if you can connect to the Internet, you can meet and talk with creative people from every corner of the globe. What an amazing possibility this is. Think of the endless opportunity our connectedness provides.

Write down your "aha moments."

Many great opportunities are fueled by "aha moments." These can be funny, amazing, and insightful times that alter your perspective. They may be insights about what you do or don't want. They can also be surprises contrary to what you have thought you are capable of. Carry a small notebook with you and document these moments that take you by surprise and reveal something interesting. They can be such things as opportunities that suddenly seem to appear or insights you gain from others. You will find endless opportunity to create things from these moments of clarity and discovery.

Keep a journal to work out issues you struggle with.

Some people say there is no such thing as a problem; there are only opportunities. I concede from my own experience that they are right. For every problem or issue, there is a solution; and the solution will have value for your own personal growth and the growth of others. Documenting obstacles, problems, and the solutions you use to overcome them is an opportunity for you to bring value to others. Those you meet will give you value based on their understanding and experience, and it should be reciprocal—you can offer them value from those issues you've overcome.

Be accepting of unique and "out-of-the-box" ideas.

If your first reaction to an idea is defensive, stop yourself and think, "Wait, listen, let them finish." Listen to the entire idea and then imagine the possibility of it. Don't shoot down an idea just because it sounds far-fetched or strange. Give it a moment, wait for your defensiveness to pass, and then look at it again. Sleep on it or wait several days to get your prejudices out of the way. It has taken years of persistence for me to accept several unorthodox ideas that have proven valuable. Often our rejection is a habit; we don't really even think things through as we are in such a rut of rejecting everything.

AFFIRMATION
I AM SO HAPPY AND GRATEFUL TO RECOGNIZE
AND ACT ON GREAT OPPORTUNITY.

Evict limiting beliefs and mindsets.

Are you one of those people who say, "I'm just not that creative"? Do you think playing with gadgets is frivolous? Are you a bit too serious? Are you easily offended? Are you willing to indulge your curiosity, or are you afraid of looking foolish? Do feel a need to follow the rules without question? All these things come from limiting beliefs and mindsets, which limit your ability to sense opportunities. Identify and evict your limiting beliefs from your life. Often, these ideas are just reflections of things we were told as young people—such as, "You're not smart with money," or, "You can't just jump off a cliff and expect to fly." Take the time to honestly evaluate what's being presented rather than reacting.

Express your gratitude.

Gratitude is the antidote to resentment and complacency. Resentment and complacency block your ability to see situations clearly. The best way to clear resentment and complacency from your mind is to be grateful for where you are right now. Be grateful for your gifts and your weaknesses. Be grateful for your successes and your setbacks. If you are grateful for all things, including those that appear to go wrong, you will be able to see them for the opportunities they are.

CHAPTER 16
POSITIVE MENTAL ATTITUDE

CHAPTER 16

POSITIVE MENTAL ATTITUDE

I am creating positive energy in my life every day.

Have you checked your attitude lately? If you know you have an upbeat and positive attitude about life, congratulations! Maybe that's not your case, however you don't think your attitude is all that bad. If you want to get honest about your attitude, ask yourself this question: "If I were shopping at Costco and saw my attitude for sale on the shelf, would I buy it?" If the answer is no, and you would continue shopping for a different attitude, which one do you think would serve you the best to get you what you want?

When you are looking at your situation in a negative way, you will not be able to see a way out of it. You will focus your attention on the problem rather than the solution. As a result, you will feel stuck and unable to move out of your current situation and fear getting into a worse predicament. Having a positive mental attitude is not about escaping reality and pretending everything is fine when it is not. Being positive is about knowing you have solutions available to you no matter what your situation is.

CHAPTER 16
POSITIVE MENTAL ATTITUDE

I am a positive person and have worked hard to be one. However, it is important to understand that I'm not positive all the time. I am continuously working to become aware of my choices, thoughts, and reactions. I frequently get asked about positive thinking, and I wanted to first clear up some assumptions about what people think it means to be positive.

Positive people are not living in a dream world with no hold on reality. Positive people may have an attitude that everything is going to work out well, but they are not necessarily unrealistic. Positive people are very capable of understanding the reality of a cynic. They just change their mindset to see the reality from a different perspective.

Have you ever heard a negative person say he isn't negative; he's just being realistic? This idea keeps people locked in a negative reality of their own creation. They believe they are protecting themselves from disappointment, not realizing they are actually attracting disappointment with their thoughts. A person's thoughts, whether positive or negative, do have an effect on his or her environment. If you think negatively, your mind will automatically seek out confirmation that the world is a terrible place. Seeing is believing, and your mind reinforces your belief that reality is negative. See how it's a downward spiral of negativity? If you expect negative results, you are less likely to take risks and try new things. Negative thinking masks your impressions in fear.

> *A person's thoughts, whether positive or negative, do have an effect on his or her environment.*

Positive thinking works the same way. With a positive mental attitude, you'll seek positive choices and expect positive results. This helps you move past fear and do things others may believe can't be done. This positive attitude typically brings about positive results. A person's thinking helps determine their reality. Negative thinking is realistic for the negative thinker, but only because their thoughts make it true. Ironically, the positive thinker also sees reality—just in a different light. Both types of people see their own reality, and both consider it **THE** reality.

AFFIRMATION
I AM CREATING POSITIVE ENERGY IN MY LIFE EVERY DAY.

Everyone who accomplishes anything—whether it's earning a million dollars or becoming an award-winning actor—accomplishes it the same way: by taking action. Positive people have the advantage because they believe the object of their desire is attainable. They come from a "can-do" mindset. Their actions are not based on fear or scarcity but rather on possibilities. Thus, a positive attitude helps a person manifest his or her desires—not simply by dreaming about it, but by inspiring the person to take action.

There is no doubt there are ugly realities to life. There are those that perceive a positive attitude ignores reality. The truth is positive thinking doesn't ignore the problem; it helps you see the problem in a new light. In fact, you don't even see problems as problems. Think about it; regardless of how you react to an external situation, the situation will still be the same. If being upset doesn't change the outcome of a past situation, wouldn't it serve you, and your health, to see the positives?

A positive mental attitude creates a mindset of abundance, enthusiasm, and solutions. Instead of thinking about what can't be done, a positive thinker will not be constrained by can and cannot. A positive thinker is free to think of new ways to solve problems because he is not limited by fear of failure. When we are in a state of abundance, we provide a fertile ground for possibilities and making dreams a reality. A positive mental attitude can—and indeed does—change reality by allowing a person to act in an entirely different way, thus harvesting entirely different results.

It's easy to believe people with a positive mental attitude have perfect lives and have never dealt with real-world hardships. Or maybe you think people wouldn't be so positive if they'd endured a few difficult times in their lives. But the truth is this is really merely a justification for negative thinking. I don't know one positive person who hasn't had real and serious trials in their life—including me. Positive people have faced disappointment, death of loved ones, physical handicap, and the whole range of human experiences we all deal with. The difference is these people didn't let those experiences change their cheerful outlook on life (or at least not for an extended period of time). A positive mental attitude means you are in control of your own thoughts and feelings.

CHAPTER 16
POSITIVE MENTAL ATTITUDE

Every person has sorrows and trials that test him to the core, but only some people have the courage to act positively and with grace through those trials. A positive mental attitude doesn't mean a person has sidestepped a hard life. It simply means they choose to see and take part in the good things life has to offer, as opposed to only the negative. Even in external circumstances that seem out of our control, we can always control our internal response. In fact, it's the only thing we have absolute control over.

There are many ways to create positive thoughts and energy in your life every day. One of my favorite ways is to meditate. I like to start my day off by meditating for ten to fifteen minutes on my affirmations first, and then I visualize myself with my goal. If any thought pops into my head that is not in alignment with what I want, I dismiss it from my consciousness. When you really get into visualizing, you will be able to feel the emotions as if you already have what you want, and you will feel gratitude for having it. Having gratitude will always create positive energy to attract what you desire.

Having gratitude will always create positive energy to attract what you desire.

Another way to create positive energy is to break your day into parts or sections and set your intention on what you want to create during each section. Decide how you are going to feel prior to going into any part of your day. The first part of your day is when you first wake up. Decide before you go to bed that you will have a good night's rest and wake up feeling refreshed and energized. Before you get out of bed, decide your process of getting ready for your day will go smoothly and with little effort. Before you get in your car and leave your home, decide your drive will be easy and flowing. As you get ready for a presentation for a client or another type of important business meeting, decide you will speak eloquently and persuasively to get the results you want. Before you come home to your family, decide you are going to spend quality time and enjoy the presence of your spouse and children.

AFFIRMATION
I AM CREATING POSITIVE ENERGY IN MY LIFE EVERY DAY.

Each new circumstance is an opportunity to practice your new mindset. You are in control of creating your desired outcomes. And as you take control, you will feel yourself becoming more and more positively energized. You will feel your mental attitude soaring to new heights. You will also have an immensely positive affect on those around you.

There are many ways to create positive changes in your mental attitude. Find the ones that work for you. Get started on it right away. There is no reason to wait. And it's so easy. It's like putting on a new set of glasses. There is nothing on the outside that needs to change in order for you to have an increase in your positive mental attitude. However, when you change on the inside, you will notice changes occurring all around you. You will see things from a different vantage point. And you will attract that which you want to see and experience in your life.

CHAPTER 17
QUALITY OF LIFE

CHAPTER 17

QUALITY OF LIFE

I expect the best quality of life.

Your life will only be as great as you can dream it to be. In order to get what you desire out of life, you must be able to imagine what you want. There are no limits other than those you place on yourself. You really can have what you want, and the fact that you may not believe this is exactly what is holding you back. When will you allow yourself to start dreaming again? Are you ready to feel all your desires bubbling up within you like when you were a child? It's all waiting for you to come and get it. Take some time to seriously evaluate where you are currently in regard to finances, relationships, health, liberty, and spirituality (not necessarily meaning religion—just your connection with your higher-self or being, or however you choose to define spirituality).

The point of this exercise is to be honest about where you are in life. This will allow you to see where you want more and what that "more" may look like. You can define exactly what you want to be and how you want your life

CHAPTER 17
QUALITY OF LIFE

to look. Now is the time to get excited about what is possible. The life you dream is yours to create. As you grow and change, so will your dreams. Right now, it may be you just want some new furniture for your living room. Once you meet that desire, you may want to refurnish the house. Once you meet that goal, you may want a brand-new house. Wanting more is human nature. It only feels bad when you think you can't have it.

For example, you may dream of having a loving, exciting, nurturing, and mutually respectful relationship but think you can't have it because your current relationship is anything but that. You may relate to Claude's story:

I was raised with an abundance of love and affection. It seemed as if I could do no wrong in my parent's eyes. Just out of high school, I married my high-school sweetheart. It was the "right" and expected thing to do. We had our first child within six months after the wedding. After thirty years of marriage, I realized I had not been happy for most of that time. At work, I was the man-in-charge. At home, however, my wife was constantly complaining and nagging and telling me nothing I did was good enough. I felt like an idiot. Life was no fun, and I was miserable. The kids were grown, and I was nearing middle age. I started to ask myself, "How much life do I have left? What level of happiness do I want for the rest of my life? Do I want to spend the rest of my life in quiet desperation?" I had to make a choice on what quality of living I wanted.

> *Do I want to spend the rest of my life in quiet desperation?"*

I ended up getting divorced. Knowing I deserved more, I chose to live a life of confidence and be in a relationship with a partner who holds me in high esteem. I wanted to have fun and feel excitement in my relationship. I met my new partner within months after my divorce. She was everything I wanted in a relationship. My new wife was raised differently, where "dad is king, and deserves respect." Being held in high esteem bestows a new level of responsibility and an urge to live up to it. I finally was in a relationship that was what I call "easy." We have so much fun together. In our nine years of marriage, we have only gone to bed mad one time. I feel like my wife is happier to see me when I get home than my dog.

AFFIRMATION
I EXPECT THE BEST QUALITY OF LIFE.

Having a supportive wife even led to me leaving a well-paying career (working hard and long hours) to go for a lifestyle I wanted with a new career of working less, which allowed me to spend more time with my family, go on vacations, and challenge myself by learning new skills. I created a whole new experience and a reality I wanted based on knowing I deserved a higher quality of life.

One of the first steps to changing your quality of life is to accept that where you are right now is the result of all the choices you have made in the past. It is important to understand how your power to choose helps you make the decisions that will turn your dreams into reality. Once you accept the responsibility for your circumstances, you can follow these steps to help make the changes ultimately leading you to success.

1. Get Clear About What You Really Want

   Without an understanding of where you are going, it's like running through a dark forest and hoping for the best. Only by focusing on what you want the end result to be, can you move in the right direction. Dreams are best met when they are fully fleshed out in your mind. Make your goals so clear you can see and feel them. Visualize the outcome and imagine how your life will be affected when it happens. As you move along in your quest, stop on occasion to see if your vision is still clear or if it needs further refinement or a new direction. This is where writing your goals is important. It allows you to see what you want on a daily basis and reminds you of how far you've come.

2. Affirmations

   After you have defined what you want in great detail, use affirmations to keep the goals clear and focused in your mind. Affirmations are extremely powerful. They can help you shift your focus from "I can't" or "I'm afraid" to "I can" and "I will." Use words or phrases to help you picture what it is you want to achieve. Be specific, keep your words in the first person, and stay positive. For example, "I am surrounded by people who value and respect me for who I am and what I do." By affirming your goals clearly in your mind, you are sending your subconscious a message that will support and encourage you. You become tuned in to those opportunities that help you meet your goal.

3. Focused Intent

Successful people are people who are motivated to stay focused on their goals. They keep their goals constantly in front of them and take specific, measurable steps to work toward those goals each day. As we've already discussed, what you focus on, you attract. When your intent is clear, you become aware of what is relevant to your life or business, and you will attract opportunities to help you.

4. Action

Make the decision to complete one step (even if it's a small step) each day to move you toward your goals. In order to do this, you must plan ahead and commit at least thirty minutes per day to outline what you will do the following day. Make a list of the items you want to accomplish and work straight through the list. Finish each item before you move on to the next. It is important to understand quality is better than quantity. You can accomplish more in thirty minutes by focusing than you can in a whole afternoon with your mind wandering.

5. Positive Attitude

As we discussed in the last chapter, a positive mental attitude is the most important key to choosing actions to lead you into the life you want. This is one area you can control at all times. Your attitude not only affects how you approach your goals, but it also determines your perspective of past events. The way we view ourselves determines our perspective on life. A positive mental attitude enhances your feelings of empowerment and makes it possible to continue moving forward, even

AFFIRMATION
I EXPECT THE BEST QUALITY OF LIFE.

when problems and obstacles appear.

There are times when we all need a good laugh, and few minutes of humor can dispel hours of frustration. Don't miss the opportunity to laugh at yourself—especially if you're taking things way too seriously. When challenges do threaten to completely overwhelm you, it is a good time to step back emotionally and give yourself a break. Even thirty minutes spent doing something enjoyable and relaxing can liberate your mind and emotions and help you return to those challenges with renewed concentration and energy. Overcoming problems will boost your self confidence, so whenever you find yourself thinking negative thoughts, stop yourself and replace those thoughts immediately with positive affirmations.

6.   Persistence

It's easy to seem like a hamster on a wheel sometimes when you keep working toward your goal, and it doesn't seem to get any closer. But don't get discouraged, it will happen. Though it may seem like you aren't making progress, you are learning and growing as a person and gathering steam to push through to your goal. Hard-won goals are the most rewarding and satisfying. Over time, you will notice you're accomplishing more with less effort. Things get a little easier. Situations don't frustrate you like they used to, and it comes from having the courage to keep trying and not give up.

Refuse to allow unhelpful criticism or negative circumstances to sway you from your goals. No matter the road you travel in life, it is all about the journey, so allow yourself to enjoy it. A successful quality of life isn't a destination; it is a state of perpetually being. The work you do, the people you meet, and the experiences you have along the way to meeting your goals are what make your life fulfilled and happy. Let your mind unlock all the possibilities. Remember you are a powerful creator. And watch as the magic happens.

CHAPTER 17
QUALITY OF LIFE

When you are living the quality of life you choose, then you have more to give to others—more to give emotionally and financially, and more time to share. It is your responsibility and privilege to raise your quality of life so you can support other people in raising theirs. Can you imagine a world where everyone is being their best and able to encourage all they meet to be his or her best as well? By raising your quality of life, you will be an integral part of making this world a better place to live in, and you will be a happier person for it.

CHAPTER 18
RELATIONSHIPS

CHAPTER 18

RELATIONSHIPS

I have an abundance of nourishing and stimulating relationships.

Think of how much your family and friends have influenced you over the course of your life. Who are the people that have supported you no matter the circumstances? Those are the people you want to surround yourself with. They play a large roll in your actions of keeping faith and believing in yourself. When you temporarily forget how great you are, they are there to remind you and support you in advancing toward your goal.

When you tell your friends about your dreams and aspirations, do they laugh at you or say you can't have what you want? Do they make statements such as, "Who do you think you are?" or, "Why do you want to do that?" What is the message being delivered either objectively or subjectively? Is this supporting you in what you want or heaping negative ideas on your party? The people closest to us can help or hurt us, depending on their own perspective and understanding. It doesn't make them bad people if they aren't supportive in the ways we would like. It only means they have their own obstacles to overcome or feel they have some reason to discourage you.

Most people don't make a conscious effort to keep other people down or prevent them from being happy. It happens unconsciously because of their own lack of self worth or fears. Many times, they may even think they are preventing you from making big mistakes. This is what happened to Jana when she received an acceptance letter and scholarship from an Ivy League school more than a thousand miles from home.

I thought my dad would be thrilled because he was so worried about paying for college. But when I told him that it was for an Ivy League school so far away, he said absolutely no way! I couldn't believe his reaction. I was hurt and upset that he seemed so supportive of me getting good grades so I could get into a nice school, but then when it happened he threw a fit. My mom finally helped me understand that no one in his family had gone to college at all so it was a big step—and this kind of school really intimidated him. Everyone he knew worked hard for a living, and he didn't feel like we were the kind of people that went to those schools, but we are—I am, and I did. Four years later, he was in the front row when I graduated and has remained my biggest fan. By proving that I could do it, he has since set some goals for himself that were way out of his comfort zone. You never know why people are the way they are, but there is always opportunity for change!

> *By proving that I could do it, he has since set some goals for himself that were way out of his comfort zone.*

So don't take it personally when you are not supported. Just share with the people you know will support you in the ways you need, and the others may eventually come around.

AFFIRMATION
I HAVE AN ABUNDANCE OF NOURISHING
AND STIMULATING RELATIONSHIPS.

I have certain family members and friends with whom I won't share some of my dreams because I know they won't support me. I am planning to move to the tropics, which has been a dream of both mine and my husband's for some time. I'm waiting until I have everything finalized before I share with them about my move. If I were to tell them now, I would have to justify my reasons for moving and then listen to them tell me all the reasons why they believe I should not make the move. They mean well, and I know they want me to stay close to them. And yet, I must keep my forward momentum moving toward my dream and stay focused on what I want, instead of what other people want for me.

Have you ever heard of a family member or long-time friend giving someone a hard time because he or she now wears a suit to work or has a great career? It happens because this person feels threatened by the fact that his friend or family member has moved up or away from him in some way. People often want to keep us the same instead of supporting change because they don't want to change. They feel badly about themselves for their lack of progress, and when you move past where you were to go for what you want, it is a reminder to them of their lack of progress. Just keep reminding yourself their thinking has nothing to do with you.

Oftentimes, reactions from those around us have more to do with their self-image than with anything else. Self-image is the personal view we have of ourselves. It is our mental image or self-portrait that has been formed by our experiences throughout life. Self-image is an internal description of the characteristics of who we are and what we are, including labels such as intelligent, beautiful, ugly, talented, selfish, and kind. These characteristics form a collective representation of our good and bad qualities as we see them. It determines what we think of ourselves and what we think we can achieve or what we think we deserve.

One interesting aspect of our self-image is we sometimes will project our own self-image onto others. For example, your sister may assume what you can or can't achieve or what you deserve based on her own self-image. She may see you as similar to her in every respect, and then if you do well and she doesn't, she may subconsciously (or even consciously) wonder what's so special about you. Why do you get all the breaks? Who did you meet that did it for you? If she were to accept that you empowered yourself and accomplished great things, it would mean the only problem she faced was with herself. And that can be extremely difficult for others—especially friends and family—to accept.

It is important to understand self-image is created through learning. Parents or caregivers make the greatest contribution to our self-image, as they are mirrors reflecting back to us an image of ourselves. Our experiences with others—such as teachers, friends, and family—add to the image we see. Relationships reinforce what we think and feel about ourselves. These experiences can produce either a real or distorted view of who we are. The image can also be positive or negative based on what we were told or learned from experience as children, and we continually adjust this image on an ongoing basis throughout our lives. We have an inner sense of our adequacy and value. With a positive self-image, we own our assets and potentials while being realistic about our liabilities and limitations. A negative self-image focuses on our faults and weaknesses and distorts failure and imperfections.

Self-image is important because how we think about ourselves directly affects how we respond to life.

Self-image is important because how we think about ourselves directly affects how we respond to life—what jobs we choose, what risks we take, and what relationships we cultivate. The good news is that our self-image is not permanently set in stone. It is always changing, and in fact, we can actively choose to change our self-image at any time. We can learn to develop a healthier and more accurate view of ourselves, thus changing the distortions we have created. A healthy self-image starts with learning to accept and love ourselves. It also means allowing others to accept and love us.

AFFIRMATION
I HAVE AN ABUNDANCE OF NOURISHING
AND STIMULATING RELATIONSHIPS.

It is interesting that when we are young, we often tend to have the same self-image as those around us. Our family and friends are very much like us, and these relationships reinforce who we are. It is not unusual for people to seek the same relationships they have known in the past—even if those relationships have been destructive or abusive. Whatever we believe about ourselves, we attract particular situations or events because they are in alignment with our self-image. A bad self-image will attract bad or unhealthy relationships. Once you shift your self-image, your circumstances will have to change accordingly.

This is why, once you decide to make a change, it is imperative that you maintain a circle of friends who will support you in your cause, whatever it may be. Your network of relationships can lift you up or bring you down. It's up to you to decide whom to share your dreams with, and you can choose to surround yourself with those who will support you. As your own self-image improves, you will attract other relationships that will continue to uplift and support you. Eventually, you will be the uplift and support for your family and friends who need a boost in their own self-image.

You can feel it when people are genuinely happy for you. Allow yourself to accept their support, and you will find yourself being propelled towards your dreams.

CHAPTER 19
SUCCESS

CHAPTER 19

SUCCESS

I am a success magnet.

The definition for success according to the Merriam-Webster Dictionary is: "1. The favorable or prosperous termination of attempts or endeavors. 2. The attainment of wealth, position, honors, or the like." That's pretty broad, so what does success look like to you? Do you look at success as the amount of money you have, the car you drive, or the clothes you wear? Or do you view success as maintaining long-term friendships, staying married for several decades, or raising children to be contributing members of society? Everybody has a different perspective on success. The important thing is to define what it means to you.

What do you see when you climb to the top of a tall mountain? Unless you are at the top of the tallest mountain, you would see another, higher peak. Generating success with your goals is much the same. Once you have achieved a particular level of success, you will more than likely want to achieve something even greater. That is how we are designed as human beings. It is in our nature to continue to want more. Success is a constant journey rather than a destination.

CHAPTER 19
SUCCESS

When I bought my first home, I felt successful. Then I looked at bigger houses in better communities. There were so many other things I wanted in a home: a larger master bedroom and walk-in closet; a pool and hot tub; a guard-gated entrance; and a game room. Each new house I lived in brought me to a new level of success. Now, I want even more specific things in a home. Feeling successful and having a sense of accomplishment with how far I have come are what encourage me to strive for more.

For many people, success used to mean sacrificing your personal and family life for your career. Now, for many of us, success means a balanced personal and professional life, which can be attained by working with more focus, alignment, and balance. It can be difficult to settle on one exact definition of success; but in order to reach any kind of goal, you must have some idea what success will look like when you get there. You may do this by using the following statements:

1. *Once I have a corporate job, I will have success.*

2. *When I can get married, I will be successful.*

3. *When I have a family, I will have achieved success.*

4. *I will be successful when we retire to the mountains.*

5. *Success for me is living in a beautiful home in Hawaii.*

6. *I feel successful when I am respected and esteemed by my colleagues.*

7. *When my book is published, I will be successful.*

All of these things are doable, but everyone looks at them differently and makes a judgment about what they perceive to indicate success.

AFFIRMATION
I AM A SUCCESS MAGNET.

Now this is not to suggest you are in any way unhappy with your life. You can be very content while striving for your next goal or next level of success. This is not to be confused with complacency. Complacency convinces us that we can maintain where we are and not need to move forward. Unfortunately, this is a lie of the mind. Because the entire world is always in motion, there is no maintaining—either you are moving forward, or you are being left behind. It is wonderful to be happy in whatever circumstances you find yourself; the danger comes when you simply settle for what life hands you and deny any interest in being, doing, or having more.

Contentment is key to living a successful life. One problem many people have is they reach their ultimate goal in life only to find they have no idea how important contentment is. Therefore, their success feels hollow and unsatisfying. Learning the fine art of contentment while refusing to be complacent will serve you well as you wrestle with issues of personal success.

So how do you create a plan ensuring your idea of success, while also providing contentment?

The first step is to describe in detail what a successful, balanced life would mean to you in ten years time (ten years is a good stretch for most people, and anything can happen in ten years if we set our minds and our hearts to it). What would your priorities be in ten years? What would be most important to you, and how would this be reflected in how you spend your time? Think in as much detail as possible—imagine the car you will drive, the house you will live in, and the vacations you will go on. Consider your work and what you will be doing ten years from now. How will you interact with your coworkers or employees? How will you balance home life and work life? Again, it is important to imagine your life right down to the minutest detail. How tall will the oak tree in your yard be in ten years? What kinds of flowers will you have in the garden? See them and smell them.

Once you've imagined your environment, then imagine what a day in your life will be like when you are living your life fully, according to the priorities you have established in the first step. In other words, how do you see the priorities

CHAPTER 19
SUCCESS

in your life fitting and working together? Are you married with small children and living a full family life? Have your children gone to college and moved away? Have you retired from your first career and perhaps embarked on a second? What do you do each day, and who do you talk to?

It is interesting how we sometimes will make statements such as, "In ten years, my business will be worth over five million dollars." But we don't really envision what that means, and we don't think about the major changes we will go through in a decade while we are achieving that success. This is why imagining how you move through the day is so important. If you have children who today are ages ten and twelve, a decade from now, one could be a college graduate, and both will be gone from home. You may be a grandparent and responsible for helping your children make ends meet.

It is easy to assume some things will move forward and then forget that the whole world changes with you. This is why the idea of maintaining your life is so unrealistic. Life goes on and moves forward whether you want it to or not; you cannot be above the relentless march of time.

A big inhibitor for success are self-limiting beliefs. In order to be successful, you must believe something is possible for you to be able to achieve it. Your beliefs are only real to you; if you think you can, you can. Conversely, if you think that you cannot, then you cannot. There is no right or wrong here; it is only right to you if you choose to believe it.

Life goes on and moves forward whether you want it to or not; you cannot be above the relentless march of time.

It is also important to have very clear, defined goals, which is the whole point of visualizing your life in ten years. If you live without goals, you accept what life offers without question and release control of your life to others. You will become lost and follow the crowd just like a sheep. Specific goals keep you focused on what you need to do and provide a clear path of action. To this end, you must have a plan with a series of goals outlined. This will allow you to develop strategies to accomplish your ultimate dreams through a series of small victories.

No matter how detailed your plan, you must put it into action. This is the most difficult part because it takes time and energy. Many people give up the moment they fail to achieve that first, small step. They may also procrastinate and never take any action, but they are always planning.

Success is a constant journey. It's not a dollar amount or an achievement. Success is your own perception and is completely dependent upon your state of mind. There are people with virtually no material wealth who feel successful. There are also millionaires who feel poor. How we feel about our accomplishments is more important than the actual accomplishment, and gratitude plays a big role in allowing you to feel successful. Being grateful for what you have and where you are in life will continue to attract more success into your life. You must recognize you are on a journey of personal growth and discovery, and your own idea of success is subject to change along the way.

It is always a good idea to take inventory of your life on a regular basis and acknowledge your successes. Allow yourself to fill with pride over your accomplishments. Even if all you acknowledge is that you want more, pat yourself on the back for taking the first step toward getting it. Each small victory leads to the next, and allowing yourself to feel the emotion of those small successes regularly leads to greater and more frequent success throughout your life.

CHAPTER 20
TIME

CHAPTER 20

TIME

I am making the best use of my time.

Time is measured in relation to the future. What isn't is more important than what is. Think of a football game. Which is more important, the score at the two-minute warning or the score that could be at the end of the game? The possible score that could be is more important. When you take a look at your current circumstances, what's more important is the life you could have, not the life you are currently living. Regardless of the life you have, you must shift your awareness to the life you want, or you will never have it.

These days, there is a great deal of attention given to the idea of time management. Everyone wants to know how he or she can fit more into his or her already-packed schedule. Actually, there is no such thing as time management because time is a static force that never changes, and you can never make more of it. The only thing you can do is to prioritize your activities

CHAPTER 20
TIME

to accomplish the things that really matter most. This may sound a little lofty, but it's an important distinction. Time management is about arranging what you do to fit as neatly as possible into the time you have available. Prioritizing, on the other hand, is about focusing only on the tasks that really matter and cutting the rest down or eliminating them altogether—and that's where it's at.

Prioritizing involves making choices and decisions about every activity you engage in to see if it adds value to your life or not. Look at your life right now, think of the activities you currently are involved in, and think about what you want to accomplish with your life. I'm sure you can probably carve out an hour or two here and there each week to work toward your goals—it may not be much, but at least it's something.

Now, imagine you went to the doctor and he told you that you had exactly one year to live. How does that change your priorities? Would you piddle around trying to accomplish your dreams in only a few hours per week? Would you work extra hours to try and get a promotion at work that would never benefit you? Would you save for a retirement that wasn't going to happen? Would you plan to take a vacation for two weeks next June and hope you made it? Would you sit in front of the TV tonight? I believe the answer is an emphatic no! Time matters in relation to how much there is, and when it's taken away, you panic.

When you think you have a seemingly unlimited amount of time, it's easy to waste it. However, when your perception is altered and artificially shortened, time becomes very precious. What many people don't realize is that time is always precious. Whether you live to be forty or ninety-something, there is still only a limited amount—and it will never seem like enough. It is for this reason that it is so important to prioritize what you do each day so your life doesn't rush past in a blur of busyness that never accomplishes anything.

Janice is in her forties and recently started her own business. She used to be a corporate executive with high-school-aged children at home.

AFFIRMATION
I AM MAKING THE BEST USE OF MY TIME.

It is amazing to me how your idea of time changes as your life changes. At one point in my life, I was sleeping less than six hours per day, putting in ten to twelve hours at work, rushing to baseball games, cheerleading practice, soccer games— you name it. Now suddenly, only three years later, the house is quiet. I work six hours per day and yet have more money, more balance, and yes, peace, for the first time in my life.

If you were to ask me what I did with all those hours, I honestly can't tell you. I know I spent a number of them each day just feeling exhausted. I wonder if I had really prioritized, how much more I would have enjoyed those years with my kids and my husband. All that time I put into a job that I really didn't care for profited me little, yet I can never get that back.

My only regret is that I didn't step back twenty years ago and decide what was important. I filled my day with mundane and useless tasks that zapped my energy and drained my desire to do more.

TIME IS A precious commodity and a non-renewable resource. We only have so much of it, and none of us knows how much we have; therefore, it would be a tragedy to waste it. The good news is everybody has the same amount of hours in a day and days in a year. This includes the people you view as extremely wealthy. If they can accomplish what they have, given the same amount of time, then you can too. You have the same ability to achieve as they do. You just have to stop living as if you have forever—you don't.

Think of your dream life. Is your current job going to give you what you want to have out of life? For many people, the answer is no. The word job stands for "just over broke." It is unfortunate how many people don't get paid what they are really worth at their jobs. Even sadder is the idea that people really believe they are only worth the price tag put on them by their employer. This is a ridiculous idea.

You have immense worth—just as much as anyone else—no exceptions. Taking this into consideration, how long are you willing to trade your time for money? You may already know you are going to have to step out of your

CHAPTER 20
TIME

comfort zone and create a business or even multiple businesses. It is only by you taking the reigns of your life that you will achieve a high degree of success. If creating your own business is not what you want, then be the best at what you are currently doing. By being the best at what you do, more doors will open for you, and new possibilities will present themselves.

Sometimes, we face tough choices involving one or more unknowns. We can't know in advance what the consequences of each alternative will be, and we can waste precious time trying to guess. This results in a great deal of lost time and stagnation. This is especially true of what we perceive to be big decisions—like quitting a job, starting a business, or moving to a new city for better opportunities. There is no way to know all the determining factors before leaping into the unknown.

Even if you feel secure in a decision, there are no guarantees. Some people don't realize refusing to make a decision is also a decision. You are trying to maintain the status quo, and as we already discussed in the last chapter, you cannot maintain. Everything moves forward—you have no choice but to also move forward or risk being left behind.

Even if you feel secure in a decision, there are no guarantees.

It is very important to be joyous in whatever you do. Life is too short to be unhappy. Often people are so intense they forget to enjoy the small things like a sunset or dinner with the family; in reality, these are not the small things but the important ones. Spend time with whom you want to spend time with and find fulfilling work in an environment you are happy to be in. Take the kind of vacations you want to take now—don't wait for "some day." Learn to play an instrument that calls to you. What really brings joy to your life? If you plan it, the likelihood of it happening will increase dramatically—whatever it is.

Cherish the time you have. You won't get it back. The most surprised people on the planet are the ones who find their names in the obituary column. As a friend and mentor of mine once said, "You are going to die." That is a true statement for everybody.

AFFIRMATION
I AM MAKING THE BEST USE OF MY TIME.

The problem is most people don't live their life that way. They do things out of obligation instead of want. They put important things off, such as telling someone how much they love them and why; spending time with their kids without being on the cell phone; making a career move; or taking their wife out on a real date. The right time is now. Take action.

CHAPTER 21
UNDERSTANDING

CHAPTER 21

UNDERSTANDING

I am accepting and understanding of myself and others.

How much do you know about you? How often do you check in with how you are feeling? Most people would argue they know themselves really well. However, just because someone may know he behaves in a particular manner, it doesn't mean he will make the changes necessary to gain a deeper understanding. Nor does it mean he will make appropriate changes to create outcomes to significantly improve his life. In order to change, a person needs a desire to change, needs the action of changing, and needs the acknowledgment of his current emotional state.

Most people I meet have a hard time answering the question of how they feel. We have been programmed to think it's what we do that is important rather than how we are feeling or being. Many people think it is what they do or don't do that makes them lovable. But this is not reality. We deserve to be loved just because we are alive. We deserve to be worthy of our wants because we are born deserving. Somehow, as small children, we get it in our heads that we are unlovable, unworthy, and undeserving. This happens because at some point, someone held back his love as a reaction to something he did or thought he should have done. This is the provenance of the story we make up about ourselves; we say we need to do or not do something in order to be worthy of attention and love.

We use our stories to protect ourselves from feeling hurt. Awareness of the mind and how we can control and direct our thoughts, beliefs, and emotions are what open new avenues of possibility. Your life becomes vastly different when you are the one directing your mind, instead of letting it direct you.

When you express love, acceptance, and respect, you feel emotions that have a high vibration, and you feel good. When you express judgments, fear, jealousy, and anger, you experience emotional chaos, which has a low vibration and makes you feel badly. The challenge is to master your emotional response to circumstances around you. You are the only one who can determine the thoughts you think, the words that come out of your mouth, and the emotions you create. Your thoughts—the choices and interpretations you have—are based on your core beliefs about yourself. When you understand how to change your core beliefs, you change the emotional quality of your life.

The power to change your life and create happiness resides within you. Happiness is a choice, and each day you can choose whether to be happy or unhappy. No one else can make you happy, and no circumstance can bring you the feeling of satisfaction you may long for. It is very common for people to think, "I'll be happy when: I get married, or I have children, or I make a million dollars, or I move to a tropical island." But the truth is none of those things can make you happy; happiness comes from within—only by really understanding your true self and using your own desire for change.

The first step in changing the way you create your life is self-awareness. Self-awareness means understanding how you think and why you do certain things. You cannot expect to change what you are not aware of. Self-awareness

AFFIRMATION
I AM ACCEPTING AND UNDERSTANDING OF MYSELF AND OTHERS.

provides the clarity to choose whether you express emotions of love or express emotions that stem from reactions to fear. This heightened awareness gives you the opportunity to catch yourself in that moment prior to saying something destructive or even thinking a negative thought. Self-awareness is the means to identify your unconscious thought patterns and raise them into your consciousness so they can be confronted and altered. It is through self-awareness that you identify and change the underlying, limiting beliefs driving your destructive behaviors, and this results in a joyful state of being.

> *Clarity allows you to perceive what is really happening instead of following the false or self-limiting beliefs in your mind.*

This understanding of self is not something you get from reading a book because we are all different. It is largely a function of perception and observation. It cannot be learned like academic subjects that fill the mind with knowledge. Understanding yourself has more to do with emptying the mind of knowledge you have learned, the preconceived ideas you have, and the previously bad experiences that have altered your perceptions. This allows us to see ourselves—and life in general—more clearly.

Emotional reactions usually stem from your assumptions about how life ought to be—not from actual events. You create assumptions about people, relationships, work, and your future. Your false assumptions (beliefs) become the setup to future emotional reactions. Self-awareness provides the presence of mind for you to see the assumptions and false beliefs before you react in a subconscious way. Clarity allows you to perceive what is really happening instead of following the false or self-limiting beliefs in your mind.

Once you have learned you have control over your emotions and practice the art of thinking before you react to situations and people, you will find you have less unnecessary emotional reactions. You can get off the emotional rollercoaster that used to take you for a ride. With practice, you can choose in the moment not to believe what your mind is telling you to be true. This

CHAPTER 21
UNDERSTANDING

allows you to see the emotional reaction coming and stop it. You can step back, allow the emotion to pass, and deal with the situation logically and calmly. You are no longer a victim to the emotions you have previously allowed to run your life. You will also be able to better understand the reactions of others who have yet to gain their own self-awareness. You may find this clarity gives you more patience and understanding of others.

Having knowledge of a personal belief or behavior and a desire to change it is not always enough. Take the smoker who knows his behavior is destructive, wants to quit, but is unable to break the habit. You may have behaviors and emotional reactions you have been unsuccessful in changing thus far in your life. In this case, what is lacking is not just awareness but personal willpower. Recovering and developing personal willpower allows you to keep your commitments with yourself and others. This is true whether the change is about addictions, emotional reactions, exercise, eating, or relationship habits. One way to recover personal willpower is by identifying and changing those core beliefs.

When you alter your perspective or get rid of limiting beliefs, you no longer commit your personal power to that idea or spend your energy on unproductive and unnecessary emotional reactions. The result is you have more energy and desire to break other habits and perceptions. With understanding and self-awareness, you not only see new possibilities for yourself and your relationships, you also have the energy and desire to make them happen. Changing false beliefs is just one way to increase your energy and happiness.

By living your life with awareness, you will also alter the way you communicate in your relationships. You will no longer express yourself through the emotional reactions that come from perceptions of the mind. You will have the choice and the desire to express yourself with love, respect, and from a responsible standpoint—instead of playing the victim. By changing the way you express yourself, people will change the way they respond to you. Relationships are where our self-limiting beliefs, emotional reactions, and lack of desire to change combine to cause the most emotional pain in our lives. Yet, relationships are where people yearn for the most change. It is the area where mastering our expression of love can have a profound impact.

AFFIRMATION
I AM ACCEPTING AND UNDERSTANDING OF MYSELF AND OTHERS.

There are many ways to approach understanding and mastering of self. All of these involve creating integrity in your mind, emotions, actions, and relationships. To accomplish this, you will need to understand and have control over your thoughts and beliefs as well as your expression of emotions. At first glance, gaining mastery over your beliefs and your emotions might appear too challenging. However, consider the alternative: letting emotional reactions from false beliefs determine the direction of your life.

Personally, I think the best way to get to know yourself is to ask yourself how you are feeling on a regular basis—and pay attention to the answer. Don't tell yourself you are fine when you're not. Constantly do an internal check-up. As you realize that you were born worthy, deserving, trusting, vulnerable, and open, and that you are able to receive and give love unconditionally, you will understand that everyone is born this way. You will experience a connection with humanity you possibly have not felt in a long time. All people want the same as you do—to love and be loved—no matter what they have or have not done.

Through this understanding, you can support others in achieving their wants and desires. Your relationships will deepen and grow. You will be able to empathize with others and effectively communicate with them. You will be kinder to yourself when you fall short of your expectations. And, in turn, you will share the same kindness with others. The worlds of "right vs. wrong" or "good vs. bad" will be substituted with effective vs. ineffective. Ask yourself, "Are the emotions I'm generating working for me or not working for me?" By answering honestly and making adjustments to your way of thinking, you will feel peaceful, and your experiences will have increased meaning.

You will continue to gain a better understanding of yourself and others throughout your entire life. As you do, you will become very clear and focused on your purpose and vision, knowing that you are important and your presence on this planet matters. You are special and have gifts only you can give to the world.

CHAPTER 22
VIBRATION

CHAPTER 22

VIBRATION

I maintain a high vibration to attract what I want.

The Law of Vibration states that everything in the universe is in a constant state of vibration. Everything in this world vibrates. All the way down to the sub-atomic level, particles are in motion. Human beings can be likened to a radio station. We put out a vibration on a certain frequency. We can also receive the vibrations other people put out when we are tuned in to the same frequency.

When you tune your radio in to 98.5 FM, you can only expect to hear what is being transmitted on that frequency. The only vibrations we can expect to receive will be on the same frequency we are vibrating on. One of the highest and most potent forms of energy is thought. Thought is electrical energy, vibrating at a very high frequency. You may have heard it said that thoughts are things. Every thought creates a vibration, which travels throughout the universe and begins to take form.

CHAPTER 22
VIBRATION

Our awareness of vibration is called feeling or emotion. When we feel down, we are putting out a low vibration. When we are in a state of gratitude or joy, we are sending out a high vibration. All of our emotions have a different frequency of vibration. There is a Law of Attraction, which is a sub-law of the Law of Vibration. The Law of Attraction states we can only receive according to our current state of vibration. If we are down and depressed, we will attract more of that emotion. If we are up and positive, we will attract more positive emotion. The question then becomes, "Are you vibrating in harmony with what you want?"

Remember, energy can neither be created nor destroyed. Therefore, the thoughts you give out exist in one form of energy or another, and will exist in some form forever. This fact means we have a tremendous responsibility to monitor and discipline our thoughts. Our thoughts form energy fields, which travel from our mind into our world. A passing thought will receive little energy, but if the thought begins to develop, and you give it attention, it carries great power. The more attention it is given, the more the thought affects or shapes our world and our relationship to it.

The Law of Attraction tells us we will draw energies to us that are similar to our own, as well as similar to whatever we focus on in our thoughts. Vibrations of similar frequencies attract one another; those of different frequencies repel one another. This is why we attract to us the things we focus on, think about, and give energy to.

> *What you think about, you will tend to bring about.*

What you think about, you will tend to bring about. When you think positive thoughts, you attract positive people and circumstances to you. When you think negative thoughts, you attract negative people and circumstances. Like attracts like. Whatever you seek is exactly what you will find. You set up the expectation in your mind, and your mind will respond. The energy you put out into the universe as a thought-form or command will draw the object of your thought to you.

AFFIRMATION
I MAINTAIN A HIGH VIBRATION TO ATTRACT WHAT I WANT.

Another sub-law of the Law of Vibration is the Law of Change, which states: because everything is energy, and energy is in a constant state of motion, everything is constantly changing. Ultimately, change is all there is. Nothing ever stays the same. This is a challenging concept for the person with limited awareness. We all know people whose security lies in everything staying the same.

Change evokes fear because it opens the door to the unknown. People will stay in bad situations just because it feels easier or safer to them than changing—they feel at least they know what is going to happen, even if it is bad. If they make a change, they enter a world outside of their realm of experience. For those with a highly-developed awareness and a broader sense of all that life can offer, riding the waves of change is much less threatening. They are more secure in themselves and have more trust, knowing somehow the universe will take care of them. To them, change may even be exciting because there is always something new—a new opportunity, a new challenge, a new gift from life.

Your rate of vibration—the kind of energy you send out to the universe—can and does change all the time. It may not seem this way; in fact, it may seem that little in you or the world changes. This is because there is a tendency for inertia to set in and for a certain pattern of vibration to repeat itself over time. Still, we can observe everything actually does change. Seasons pass, living things are born, grow, and eventually die; the economy and the weather also change, though certain cycles are repeated.

There is one major difference between human beings and the other types of examples just mentioned—we have free will, which means we have the ability to change our vibration based upon our intent. Our vibration is determined by our thoughts, beliefs, and emotions. Our emotions are actually the barometer of our vibration; they tell us the results of the vibration we are putting forth at any given moment.

CHAPTER 22
VIBRATION

Our emotions can also tend to reveal and perpetuate the thoughts and beliefs we've held in the past, which can sometimes be a trap. If we want to change something in our life, we have to break the usual pattern of thoughts and emotions. When we are feeling negative emotions, it's integral to realize this is telling us something important about our vibration and what we are presently attracting. If we can consciously remove ourselves from this negativity, even for a short time, we can at least return to a more neutral state. Then, we can focus on creating more positive beliefs that will lead to desired emotions and results.

It is very important to understand we are always vibrating some kind of energy, which is attracting something in our world. This is unavoidable—you can't turn it off and on, you can only change the frequency. We choose the thoughts we have and therefore the vibrations we send in the form of patterns of energy, which determine our experiences.

The universe is made of energy in constant vibration. Energy is never static. Everything is always changing, so we don't have the choice of freezing everything in place as it is or appears to be now. We do, however, have the choice of being in harmony with the changes. This does not mean simply being resigned to accepting the world the way it is. When we are truly in harmony with the flow of energy, we are part of it. Therefore, we are part of the choosing as to how things will work out.

There are various practices and attitudes to help us vibrate in a more positive or harmonious manner: affirmations, meditation, physical exercise, and fostering healthy relationships. One of the highest-vibration activities we can engage in is gratitude. Take a look at your life and find situations and people to be grateful for. When you allow yourself to feel gratitude for where you are currently, then you can and will start attracting more to be grateful for.

The main thing, however, is to recognize we are beings made of energy-in-motion, and we can choose our rate of vibration based on the thoughts and mental pictures we are broadcasting at all times. This means we must take responsibility for the circumstances around us, as they are nothing more or less than our own creations.

AFFIRMATION
I MAINTAIN A HIGH VIBRATION TO ATTRACT WHAT I WANT.

My husband is a commercial real-estate agent. He had a piece of land under contract to buy and needed to get the zoning changed so he would be approved for a particular project on the land. The process took months. He went before the board numerous times. It was also during the city-election time, so there was more political red tape to cut through. More than once, the outcome looked bleak. However, he kept on holding the picture in his mind of what he wanted and allowed himself to feel gratitude in advance for getting the zoning he needed. Under the circumstances, the odds for him to get the zoning were stacked high against him. He got the zoning anyway. We have no doubt he got what he desired because he aligned himself with the vibration frequency of that which he wanted. He beat the odds because of his steadfast belief in the effect of vibration.

You can achieve success in the same manner. Success occurs when you do not allow your belief to waver because of outside circumstances. The appearance of what is going on is no match for what you can create in your mind, and you allow your vibration to match that which you want. Start the practice of imagining what you desire. See yourself in possession of what you want. Allow yourself to experience what you feel as a result of having it. As you continue to allow those feelings and let go of all that are not serving your purpose, you will attract your desires to you.

CHAPTER 23
WILL

CHAPTER 23

WILL

I am engaging my will to focus on my heart's desire.

The will is used to fuel a burning desire. People have used their will to commit atrocities, and they have used it to make the world a better place—and everything in between. You can will yourself to do anything when your desire is strong enough. All it takes is commitment.

Every person has made mistakes and has committed acts he or she is not proud of. You must forgive yourself for those things. They were lessons for you to learn. It is important to understand that will gives you choice. If you do not want to feel embarrassed, shameful, or any other negative emotion, then you can choose to will yourself to feel proud, gracious, or happy. The important thing is to commit to the future and what it is you desire. Use your will to let the past be the past—without losing the lessons gained.

CHAPTER 23
WILL

Combining your will with commitment will allow you to accomplish your goals. Let's say someone said he would give you one million dollars if you would cross the street one thousand different ways. Would you find one thousand different ways to cross the street? Yes, you would. You may have to get creative, however you would find a way. One hundred percent commitment—backed by your will—produces results every time. You make the decision, and you make it happen. Use your will when the going gets tough. When you don't think you can make it to the finish line, stick to your commitment. The harsh truth is whatever your results are, that's what you are committed to. The only thing standing between you and what you want is your will and commitment.

Do you find yourself saying or doing the same, ineffective, and negative things repeatedly? You aren't alone. Many people feel trapped, like actors in a movie, rather than authors of their own lives. Feeling this way hides the fact we can choose to change. We can identify the negative thoughts and beliefs in our lives, and we have the power to change them. However, change cannot take place unless we become active participants in our own lives.

Change cannot take place unless we become active participants in our own lives.

I encourage you to do the following: make a list of five things you want to be different in your life and next to each item write down whether someone else has to change first for you to achieve your goal. If you discover your happiness is based on another person changing first, whoever that person may be, you might be waiting a long time to become happy. No one else can ever make you happy. Therefore, it is highly likely you will become increasingly stressed during the wait. You will lash out at others and berate them for not living up to your expectations of happiness. You will be surrounded by stress and chaos as you become even unhappier because things are not working out as you want them to.

AFFIRMATION
I AM ENGAGING MY WILL TO FOCUS ON MY HEART'S DESIRE.

The only way you will feel empowered is if you focus your time and energy on what you can do differently to improve particular situations. This means using your will to commit to what you want and taking responsibility for change. This does not mean others can't or won't help you. In fact, empowered individuals develop satisfying relationships in their lives. A cornerstone of such relationships is the capacity to be empathic and to place yourself in the shoes of others and see the world through their eyes. To become more empathic, ask yourself, "In everything I say or do, what do I hope to accomplish? Do I say or do things in ways that will motivate others to be willing to listen and respond to me? Do I behave towards others in the same way I would like them to behave toward me?" Make a list of the words you would like people to use to describe you and then list the words you think they would actually use. Reflect upon what actions you might take to change your behavior so the two lists align more closely.

The ability to express yourself and communicate with others is an important part of making these big changes and is closely linked to empathy. Effective communication includes an appreciation of how our verbal and nonverbal messages are perceived by others and our capacity to be an active listener. Active listeners attempt to understand what the other person is expressing, and even if they disagree, they are respectful and validate that they "hear" the other person's viewpoint. The more effectively we learn to convey our feelings, thoughts, and beliefs verbally and nonverbally, the more successful we will be in achieving our goals and staying committed.

If you are to nurture your will and make it stronger, you must learn to accept yourself. Acceptance means having realistic expectations of yourself and your goals and recognizing your strengths as well as your shortcomings. This will help you in learning to lead an authentic, balanced life in which your behaviors are in accord with your values and goals.

It is difficult to maintain our commitment and will if we do not nurture connections with people from whom we gather strength. In addition, our own empowerment will be enhanced if we serve as a source of strength and support for others. In this regard, consider the following questions: Who are the two or three people who serve as positive influences in my life? What have they done that has prompted me to list them in this way? What people would say I am the positive influence in their lives, and why? Aside from relationships with people, what other activities in my life supply me with a sense of connectedness? In what ways am I compassionate and giving? Being connected to and helping others provides meaning to our lives and serves to boost our confidence and positive attitude.

You may be thinking, "Well, easy for you to say. It's not like you have made the same big blunders I have." Not true. I've made my share—in fact, everyone has; it's how we learn. However, the ways in which we understand and respond to mistakes and failures are an integral part of developing a positive mindset. When you make a mistake, what do you tell yourself? How do you react? It would better serve all of us to consider mistakes as experiences for learning and growth. Ask yourself, "What can I do differently next time in order to succeed?"

Those with a negative mindset typically interpret mistakes as attributable to conditions that cannot be easily corrected, such as a lack of intelligence. They feel defeated by mistakes and often end up blaming others, quitting, or refusing to attempt new things. Observe what you say to yourself when you make a mistake. It will give you a clue about how you talk to yourself and what you might have to change.

Just as we have to learn to respond to setbacks in a positive way, it is also important to understand how to react to successes in our lives. Think about how you understand your achievements. Those who are positive and empowered view their accomplishments as based upon their own resources and strengths—this is an obvious result of their will.

In contrast, people who are negative tend to attribute any success to factors outside their control such as luck, chance, fate, or they dismiss their success altogether. Consequently, they are not as confident or optimistic about being successful in the future. Each one of us has particular things we do well. Focus on those things to build your confidence and then go for something new. Having some short-term successes will give your will a boost.

AFFIRMATION
I AM ENGAGING MY WILL TO FOCUS ON MY HEART'S DESIRE.

Self-discipline and self-control play a significant role in our daily activities. When we think before we act, consider the feelings of others, reflect upon possible solutions to problems, behave in a rational and thoughtful way, and engage in writing our goals, we are displaying self-discipline and self-control. These are major components of invoking our power and will upon ourselves. Self-discipline and self-control must be exercised in the following ways: accept ownership for your behavior; be consistent but not rigid; become a proactive problem solver—think of different solutions before you act; believe that every problem has a possible solution; and remember that with effort and patience, possible solutions become probable solutions. It is difficult to be truly empowered and have satisfying relationships if you are impulsive, arbitrary, and unpredictable.

If we abandon well-established diets and exercise, our health will suffer. The same principle is true if you set out to live an empowered life and then fail to see your commitments through. You cannot settle back and assume these improvements will be maintained on autopilot. Expected and unexpected challenges will emerge that test your ability to overcome. You must constantly focus on what you want in order to achieve it.

You must ask yourself, "What's more important?" What you say you are committed to—or your excuses for not having it? We have our reasons and we have our results. Our results tell us exactly what we are committed to. Are you going to keep letting your excuses get in the way of what you want? Just reading this book is a good sign you are not. But it takes more than just reading. It takes action. What tools from this book have you implemented into your life? If you haven't started implementing any, there is no better time than now. Draw forth your will and take a step. Keep using your will until you form a habit. It takes approximately thirty consecutive days to form a new habit. Once you have formed healthy, new habits, you are well on your way to a life of liberty and an abundance of wealth.

You are in charge of your will. Put it to work for you—regarding your health, relationships, finances, and spiritual connection. You have an endless supply of power with the use of your will. Go ahead, the world is waiting for you to just simply commit to what you want and get started.

CHAPTER 24
THE "X-FACTOR"

CHAPTER 24

THE "X-FACTOR"

I am unlocking my "X-factor."

In the world of mathematics, an "x-factor" is an unknown quantity, which only becomes known after following a prescribed process. You also posses an "x-factor," which shows itself when you apply the principals found in this book. The x-factor is what separates you from the rest of the crowd. You are unique in many ways. The talents you posses are unlike any other.

What is your unique gift? Do you have a way with words? Do you have an eye for finding beauty all around you in an artful way? Are you able to connect with people easily? Think about what makes you special. You may find it in what you are passionate about. Believe in the greatness of yourself no matter what image you see in the mirror. Eventually, you will see your magnificence in the reflection.

CHAPTER 24
THE "X-FACTOR"

No matter how hopeless a person may seem to be, everyone has the ability to achieve astounding heights. You have a connection with infinite intelligence. All it takes is a willingness to tap into it. Visualize what you want every day. Allow yourself to get into a higher vibration by having an abundance consciousness and using creative-thinking methods. Give yourself the freedom to make mistakes and learn the lessons. Keep your intention set on your goals. Know that every cloud does have a silver lining if you are willing to look for it.

Mike had forty-four jobs before he was twenty-two years old, and he had failed at many of them while he searched for what he had a passion and talent for. During his early twenties, Mike worked three jobs at the same time to make ends meet. It would have been easy to say he was doing all he could do to have a good life. However, he always knew he deserved better and life didn't have to be so hard. His intention was set on the life he wanted to have. He committed to finding his niche in the business world to create an abundant lifestyle.

Mike found his "x-factor" in his unique ability to connect with people. He now develops immediate rapport by making people feel at ease with his quick wit and great sense of humor. He took many risks and found his niche in real estate. It wasn't always easy. There were times when he lived off his credit cards, knowing the big deal would eventually come in. The deals did come. His thoughts were in alignment with what he wanted. Worrying about his current circumstances was a waste of time. Moving forward into his dreams is how he created his success. Not only has his "x-factor" paid off in millions of dollars, he now also has a more fulfilling family life—with a wonderful wife and the happiest children I've ever been around.

When you think about talent, you might think of Michael Jordon or Oprah Winfrey. But do you see yourself as talented? Talents are your innate abilities. Your talents are not the same as your job, your skills, or your education. You were born with your talents. If any of you have children, you quickly see they're born with different talents. Some like to dash around the house and climb fences. Others prefer to sit and draw or engage in conversation with people.

AFFIRMATION
I AM UNLOCKING MY "X-FACTOR."

You may change jobs, positions, and roles—but your talents go with you. Your talents show up at work, with friends, at church, in the community, and when you're socializing, playing, working, or relaxing. Your talents are always with you.

The work and activities you gravitate toward reveal your talents. I have a friend whose talent is organizing, and she has helped me out on occasion. She is amazing at keeping her files, closets, and supplies in order. Her closet-organizing skills are most exceptional. She'll spend hours hanging clothes just right and separating her shirts from sleeves to no sleeves, solids to stripes to prints, and then by color. When I asked her why she spends so much time, her response was, "I enjoy doing it. It relaxes me." Organizing is clearly her talent. To discover your talents, simply ask yourself, "What do I enjoy doing? How do I like to spend my time? What comes easily and effortless for me?"

Your greatest strength can also be a weakness. For instance, if you like to plan ahead, this is a great talent. But when circumstances require flexibility and spontaneity, you might not respond easily. The sales person who is good at penetrating new accounts may be lousy at daily account management. Every talent has value—but not in every situation.

Sometimes, you can ask others to immediately point out your talents, but often you have talents that are not quite so obvious. One way to find these talents is to ask these questions to individuals who are close to you: "What do I do that bugs you? What do I sometimes do to excess?" Then flip their answer around and look for the positive side of this quality. When you walk into a room, do you see every problem and issue needing to be fixed? Then you might have a talent for detail and problem solving. Do others tell you you're a Pollyanna and your head is in the clouds? You might be an optimist. Choose the right time and place to use your talent strengths and look to see how these talents will help you.

No matter how many talents you have, one of them is a primary talent. This primary talent is a driving force in your life. If this talent is missing, you'll lose the fire in your belly. We can see this happen to the entrepreneur whose company is sold. The person loses steam when they're not at the helm and taking risks. If there's no need for our primary talent, or if it's not valued, we lose our oomph for what we're doing. Our primary talent is the one that motivates us to use all the rest.

We all have five to seven core talents that we use in a predictable way to get things done. How you orchestrate these core talents is your own, personal success pattern. A success pattern is the unique way you mix and match your talents to achieve your goals. You may want to research a project before jumping into action. On the other hand, another person might prefer to jump in feet first to figure things out on the fly. Respect these differences—especially because we tend to choose partners whose talents balance our own. This can either be a source of ongoing frustration or a unifying force as the two of you team up to compliment each other's strengths and minimize weaknesses.

When you use these talents to your advantage and your dream starts to become reality, numerous good things come at you all at once. Not only did Mike make the money he wanted, he has multiple homes, the liberty to take the vacations he wants, his children are the happiest and most pleasant I've ever been around, and he has a great relationship with his wife. Not only have he and his family benefited from his success, the world around him has also profited from all he has given to charity and his general good-heartedness he shares with all whom he meets.

Your dream starts to become reality, numerous good things come at you all at once.

This highlights another truth. Once you discover your true talent and take the steps to live your passion, you will be successful. Those who experience success and abundance often want to give back—and not just because of what others will think of them. Giving back feels good. It enhances your feeling of achievement and gives you the assurances that not only are you helping yourself, you are also helping those around you. This gives you tangible evidence that you are on the right path. It gives you something to feel proud of, and those great feelings encourage you to do even more.

AFFIRMATION
I AM UNLOCKING MY "X-FACTOR."

One of the greatest contributions successful people can make is to help others find their own x-factor, to encourage them to find their own unique talents, and to strive toward their own passion in life. Often, entrepreneurs will volunteer in schools to mentor young people. Can you imagine if someone had encouraged you to follow your talents and dreams at the age of fourteen? We are taught reading and writing, but we aren't taught to believe in ourselves or understand our talents. When you give the gift of encouragement and confidence to someone, you are changing his or her life, and that cannot be underestimated.

I've spent several years giving my time to help others understand how to believe in themselves and empower their lives. It is something I will never forget, and I know many of them changed their lives because of it. No matter what I may go on to accomplish, or how successful and abundant my life becomes, I will always cherish the times when I've helped someone else understand his potential and live his dreams.

Your dream may and probably will look different from mine. Whatever you want for yourself is wonderful. That's the best part. You get to decide the life you want. It's not being selfish to want a grand life. The more you have and the better you feel, the more you'll have to share with the world. It is your duty and privilege to create a life of wealth and abundance and then share your encouragement and knowledge with others.

CHAPTER 25
YOU HAVE ALL YOU NEED

CHAPTER 25

YOU HAVE ALL YOU NEED

I have all the resources needed to create my wealth and liberty.

Everything you need in order to have a life of wealth and liberty is inside you. There is nothing external to fix your life and make it all better. There is no fairy dust to sprinkle on you. You've probably heard the saying, "If you're looking for a helping hand, look down at the end of your sleeve." There is much truth to that statement.

It's time to put what you know into practice. If you've just been reading this book without applying any of it to your life, there's no better time to start applying than right now. Go back through the chapter titles. Which ones call to you? What do you want to implement first? You don't have to go in any particular order. Okay, minimum participation is to start with your affirmations. If you do not have your own, there is an affirmation at the beginning of each chapter. Pick two or three affirmations that serve you best at this time. You'll know they're the right ones because you won't believe

CHAPTER 25
YOU HAVE ALL YOU NEED

them as being true right now. That's okay. Now, make a commitment to say them out loud a minimum of three times a day for thirty days. It may seem awkward at first. However, at the end of the thirty days, you'll have a completely different perspective.

Yes, it can be this simple to attract wealth into your life. It takes so much more effort to keep it away. As your beliefs about you begin to change, you will apply more of the principles in this book without even consciously thinking about it. Applying these principles will flow naturally for you because you'll be removing your disempowering beliefs that are standing as roadblocks. Don't be surprised by your new reality; you created it. Remember to be grateful for all the good that comes to you.

So you're saying your affirmations, but now what? Here are a few steps to help launch your new life:

1. Set your goals.

   If you don't know what you want, how are you supposed to get it? Many people know what they don't want, but that does not help them to get what they do want. You must think about how you want your life to be and write down those goals. Walking through life with a clear understanding of what you don't want is not sufficient to empower yourself. It is like going shopping with a list of items you don't want to buy. It can help to keep you away from the things you don't want, but it does not help you to get the things you do want. Decide what you want and make a list.

2. Identify the potholes.

   The potholes are your excuses. What is keeping you from having your perfect life? Do you think you aren't smart enough? You are. Do you think you don't deserve success? You do. Are you afraid of change? Everyone is. Just do it. The bottom line is you are in control of you.

AFFIRMATION
I HAVE ALL THE RESOURCES NEEDED TO CREATE MY WEALTH AND LIBERTY.

Identify these beliefs that keep getting you off track and fill in those potholes.

3. Face your fears.

I have to admit, I have my own doubts and anxieties at times. But the important thing is to know how to deal with them. When you feel yourself having a needy moment, stop—and find your center. You do this by finding a moment of peace and quiet; close your eyes and internally visualize yourself achieving your goal. See, hear, feel, smell, and taste what it is like to achieve that which you are after. Make it even more real by intensifying the sounds and colors in the movie of your mind. If the idea of achieving this goal does not fully satisfy you, make adjustments to it and rerun the vision until you are fully satisfied and have expelled any doubt of this being the right goal for you.

4. Deal with your limiting beliefs.

This can be a bit tricky, because some of our limiting beliefs about our self, others, and the world stem from the distant past and are hard to uncover. When you identify a limiting belief, step back and look at it as objectively as possible. Ask yourself the following questions:

- *Is this the truth?*

- *Do I know for an absolute fact it's the truth, or is it my perception?*

- *Is this belief serving me?*

- *How do I reverse this belief to one that does serve me?*

- *What affirmation will I say to combat this belief?*

Once you spot the culprits, it is much harder for them to have control over you. Why? Because you are really the one in control, and you are now aware of it.

5. Evaluate where you are.

How did you get where you are, and what keeps you there? Of course, there are different strategies people employ to maximize happiness, and not all of them are successful. But the agenda is pretty much universal—we all want to be happy, and we also don't want to suffer. When we perceive we might suffer or something might be hard, it becomes very easy just to stay with the status quo.

As controversial as it sounds, if you have been stuck in an unhappy situation for a while, whether it is a job, relationship, or whatever, it is likely you are getting something out of it—because otherwise, you would have moved on.

For example, I know a business woman who was transferred to a new position, which meant she had to travel around the world constantly. After a little while in this new position, she gained thirty pounds though she had been trim for more than ten years. She was confused about this because she had lost a tremendous amount of weight in her twenties and had given up her addiction to food. So why did she start gaining weight?

Later, she realized she had done it because it made it easier for her to socialize. In a job where she only spent short periods of time with a constantly changing group of people, many of their meetings were over meals, and eating was a way of connecting. Once she realized why she had started eating again, she soon lost the weight. Learning how to socialize with others was the challenge she had to face and overcome.

AFFIRMATION
I HAVE ALL THE RESOURCES NEEDED TO
CREATE MY WEALTH AND LIBERTY.

If you want to move toward your goal, you have to first be clear on what you would like to keep from your present situation. Change for change's sake does not last. If you want to make a change in your life, make sure you keep the best aspects of your current situation and discard all the aspects you do not like.

6. Baby steps.

Don't bite off more than you can chew, but make sure you do take a bite to get yourself started toward your goal. It is okay to start small, and those little successes give you the confidence and encouragement to keep going. Move at a pace challenging yet comfortable for you—but not too comfortable—otherwise you will fall back into your stagnating comfort zone. As you start to invest time and energy in your goal, you will find it quickly starts to change you as a person, your relationships, and your priorities. And last, but not least, your goal itself will start to change. Yes, that's right, as you are going after your goal, it will start changing, maybe a little, maybe a lot; but it will definitely change. It is helpful for you to understand this is a natural and productive process.

Stay calm as all these changes unfold in front of your eyes, and trust yourself. With calm persistence, you will reach your goal, even if it ends up looking very different from what it looked like when you first began.

7. Give back.

Set goals to benefit you, and they will. But also set goals involving some degree of unselfishness by trying to add benefit to others. This has to do with stretching yourself. If you do not feel a little unsure of yourself, maybe even a bit uncomfortable and challenged, chances are you are not living up to your potential.

CHAPTER 25
YOU HAVE ALL YOU NEED

You are actively choosing to embark on a journey into the unknown, where you become a tool for a higher purpose. It requires of you a certain degree of surrendering to the universe, divine power, God, or whatever label you put on a higher consciousness.

You are important, and you matter. Your presence makes a difference on this planet. You get to decide the difference you want to make. Nothing you desire is too big or too small. Remember your ideal picture of wealth. Take some time to focus on it. No matter the sizes of your dreams—go for them. Why? Because you can. Call forth from within whatever you need to make it happen.

CHAPTER 26
ZEAL

CHAPTER 26

ZEAL

I am zealous in my efforts.

Think back to the last vacation you planned. Were you excited and enthusiastic about all the details? Most people spend more time planning a vacation than they do planning anything else. They imagine where they will go, what they will do. They look at the options for activities, restaurants, and sights they want to see. They go on the vacation because their excitement and zeal carried them through to their desired outcome: the vacation. Just like the excitement of planning a vacation, it takes sustained effort to manifest all your wants and maintain that excitement and passion. This is called zeal.

Zeal has gotten a bad rap in the past as it was used to describe holy wars or terrorist excitement. But that's not really what zeal means. Zeal is a knowledgeable understanding and excitement about the future. It is not blind fervor or an overexcited and misplaced set of ideals. Zeal is leaping out of bed in the morning, grateful to be alive, and looking forward to following your passion throughout the day.

CHAPTER 26
ZEAL

People lose sight of their dreams because they spend more time worrying about the how or why they don't already have what they want. Their focus is misdirected. Some fall into the trap of fearing success and don't capitalize on their zeal. They think if they actually succeed, then they will have the responsibility to maintain a certain level of success. Others feel comfortable with being a great "number-two" person, staying out of the limelight and not sticking their neck out. There is nothing wrong with living this way if you are truly happy with it. However, if you want more, you must take a risk and get out of your comfort zone. You must allow your excitement to bubble forth and help you rather than denying its existence.

It's time to create a new belief system. Let go of and overcome your limiting beliefs about how much you deserve, and go for what you want. Creating a new belief happens by applying what you know. Tell yourself over and over how truly magnificent you are. Keep saying your affirmations daily. Taking action starts with how you think. Develop new habits of positive self-talk. Before you know it, you will believe what you are saying and will have tangible results to back up your new belief system.

> *Let go of and overcome your limiting beliefs about how much you deserve, and go for what you want.*

Fulfilling your purpose will require passion (zeal, fervency, or enthusiasm). "Purpose" has to do with our head—thinking about why we're here and understanding our calling. Passion has to do with our heart—the internal fire motivating and energizing us to fulfill our purpose. In the world we live in, natural passion is often a key to success and impact. Knowing information is valuable, but possessing the fire is invaluable. Nothing major in history was ever accomplished without zeal. It is the deciding difference between successful and unsuccessful people in every field. The fire on the inside affects everything on the outside. William Ward once said, "Enthusiasm and persistence can make an average person superior; indifference and lethargy can make a superior person average."

AFFIRMATION
I AM ZEALOUS IN MY EFFORTS.

Passion is not something that is static or that stays the same. A fire either spreads or burns out. The tendency of fire, if left alone, is to go out. Passion works the same way. We need to work it, stoke it, and build it. There are many passion killers. A few common ones include complacency, difficult circumstances, an unbalanced lifestyle, and familiarity. The result is apathy. Apathy isn't a state of mind; it's a state of heart. Our feeling is the moment we lose our passion or zeal, we lose vision and perspective. The result is we live lukewarm lives within the bounds of our comfort zone and never find out what could have been—though we often wonder. Don't think just because you may deny your dreams today and pretend they don't exist, they won't surface as regrets later. They will. Guard the flame within you and protect your passion.

The best way to maintain your zeal is to be around others who have the same zeal. Get involved in a mastermind group or employ a life coach. I refer to this as "filling the well." You can't feel upbeat if you are constantly stressed and overburdened with life. How many times have you gotten together with friends when you were feeling totally exhausted—and after an hour or two of laughs, conversation, and ideas—you felt energized and ready to take on the world again?

Cut yourself some slack. Allow the time to refill your own well and treasure the time with those who energize and excite you. Over time, this will be something you can do for others. Understand your purpose and then seek to fulfill that purpose with passion, and pursue it relentlessly. Focus your passion on fulfilling your purpose.

Take this opportunity to change, grow, serve, and reach out. Living abundantly is about living with a sense of urgency and passion. It's living with a vision and a dream to devote our lives to and achieving the goals that will forever change us.

CHAPTER 26
ZEAL

We're living in extraordinary times. The old answers don't serve anymore—in fact, our biggest challenge may be discovering the questions. A life coach in your corner assures a smoother ride and encouragement during the tough times. Ask yourself these following questions:

- Am I living by deadlines instead of living my passion? Living your passion is living by intention.

- Am I out of touch with the people, places, activities, and energies that feed my spirit? These are the things that will serve your future.

- Am I committed to finding the resources—social, emotional, financial, and spiritual—to move forward in the direction of my dreams?

- Am I ready to persevere and set aside the fears and limiting beliefs standing in my way?

NO ONE SAID life was going to be easy. However, it doesn't have to be difficult, either. The fear of reality is always much more intense than reality itself. We imagine a much worse outcome than is even possible in order to make us feel better about staying right where we are and not changing.

We make our lives into whatever we choose. Actively embrace the life you have dreamed about. Pursue your wants with diligence. Never give up on you, no matter what challenges come your way. Enjoy the journey.

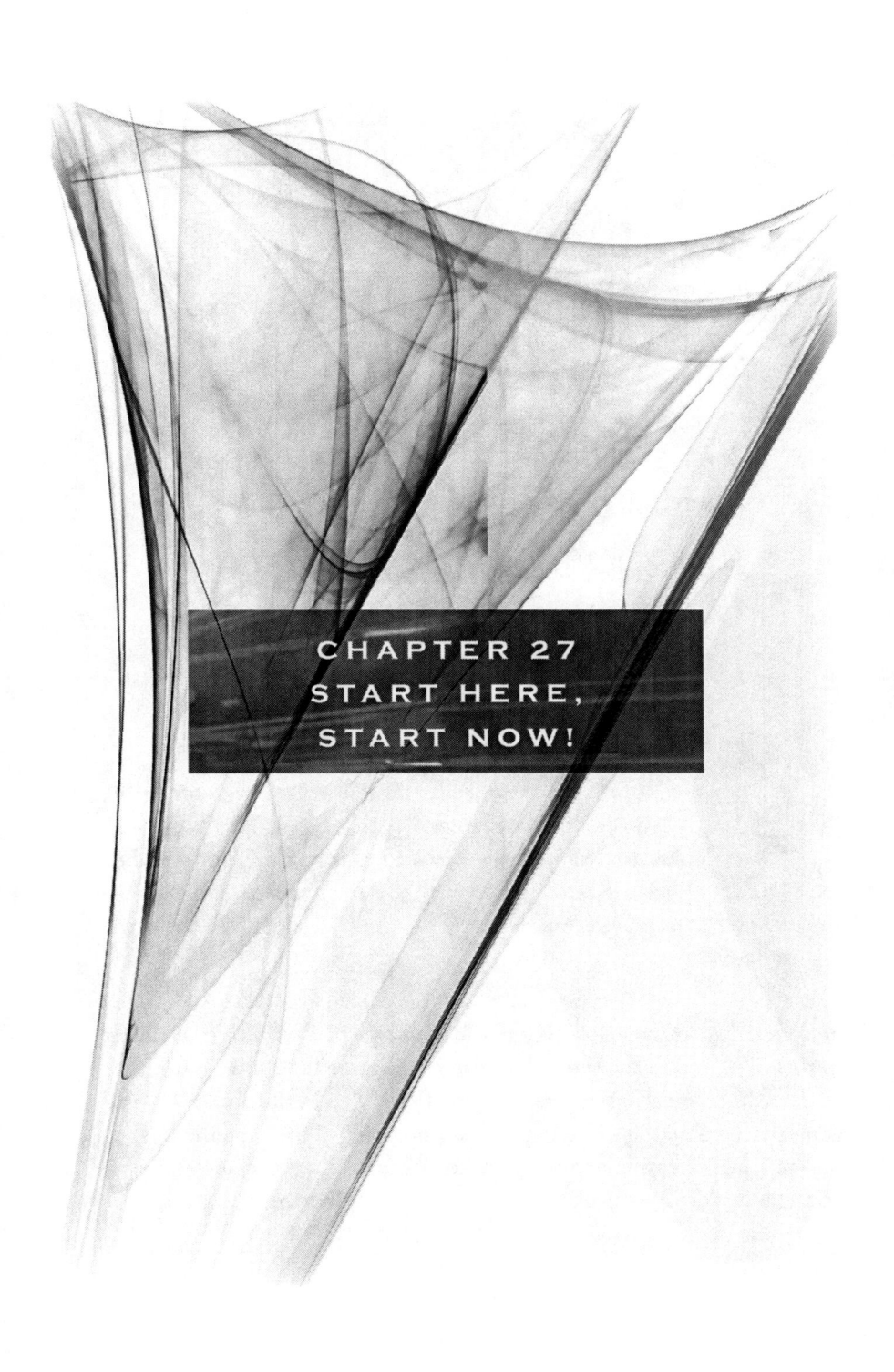

CHAPTER 27
START HERE, START NOW!

CHAPTER 27

START HERE, START NOW

Enjoying your journey

As you've probably heard, life is a journey, not a destination. You may have just started on your path of personal growth with this book; or possibly, you've been on this path for years. Either way, persistently keeping on with your learning is essential. Take some time to reflect on how far you've come. Acknowledge yourself for where you are right now.

You are truly an amazing being who is capable of achieving whatever you desire. The power each one of us possesses is incredible and unique. It's time to start implementing the techniques found in *Wealth Magnetz*. The first action step to take is choosing and saying your "I am" statements out loud several times a day. There is no more powerful way to change your beliefs about yourself. Congratulations if you've already started!

Notice if you're still saying to yourself, "It sounds too easy." Yes, it does sound easy. You may feel it's not enough effort to change your circumstances. However, if you are not doing it, you'll never know the difference it makes in your life. By putting this simple exercise into practice, you will be changing your behavior. This is by no means an easy feat. People are generally resistant to change. You will break out of the norm and have a different life experience. Give it at least thirty days. I'd love to hear and share your testimonial of the difference it made in your life. You can share your story at www.wealthmagnetz.com.

Once you've created a new habit with your "I am's," you can start implementing other *Wealth Magnetz* strategies. What product or service have you wanted to share with the world? What difference have you wanted to make? Clearly define what it is you want. Then take action. Action is needed for any plan to work. Break your goal down into doable tasks and yearly, monthly, and daily actions and results that are needed. Gather a team of people who will support you in what you want. Don't share your dreams with people who won't support you. In the early phases of your dream action plans, your dreams are fragile as a new sapling. They need to be nurtured with positive thoughts and actions to become as strong as an oak tree. Design your team to support you in this. Have your team hold the picture of the perfect end result.

Remember to have fun along the way. Your team can support you in this. Ask for what you want. No one truly makes it all alone. Support is always needed at some level. A personal coach is a great resource for support. Enjoy your journey. Life is too short to hold off on the little pleasures until later. Take some time on a regular basis for you to rejuvenate your soul. Recharge your batteries when you need to. And definitely lighten up on yourself. Don't take yourself so seriously. There is no fun in that. Besides, it's easier to attract support if you can have and be fun.

I'd like to leave you with these words inspired by one of my mentors, Jack Lannom, motivational speaker and author of *People First:* "I am proud of you for challenging yourself to be the best you can be. I believe you can and will make a difference in the world. I need you to believe in yourself as I do. Thank you for your trust and allowing me into your life through my words. And lastly, when in doubt, the answer is YES! You Expect Success!"

NOTES

My Purpose Partners

The following pages contain contact information of businesses I have used and recommend to support you in creating an abundant and wealthy life. Please consider them in your search for aid in creating your dreams.

MMS Institute, LLC
Coaching change successfully since 1974

THE ORIGINAL COACH TRAINING!

MMS supports you in making your visions and goals become reality...
We do this in a variety of ways...Globally...
Virtually...Online...DVDs...Books

- **MMS Worldwide Online Coaching Community:**
  Find a coach, learn about coaching, become connected!
  www.drcheriecoaching.com
- **MMS Virtual Training: Online 24/7**
  www.mmsvt.com 12 Coach Training Classes plus
  7 Management Development Courses
  In the convenience of your home or office
- **MMS Coach Training: The "Original" Coach Training!**
  Become a Certified MMS Coach!
  www.themms.com or www.themms.eu
  12 weeks of Personal Development plus Coaching Skills
- **Inner Negotiation Workshop: Journey to the Center of the Self**
  Breakthrough old habits, for those who
  want BIG results in very little time. Two days to
  Transform Your Ability to Manifest the Life You Want
- **Licensing to Teach MMS Courses**
  In your area of the world www.themms.com
  Our courses have a track record of 35 years
  33 Courses, Six Options to Choose
  from, 12 in Management Development
- **MMS Trainers Master Class for MMS Coaches**
  Become one of our Certified MMS Leaders
  www.themms.eu
- **Books, DVDs, CDs, Posters, Inspirational Cards**
  www.drcherie.com and buy in our online store

CREATE WEALTH

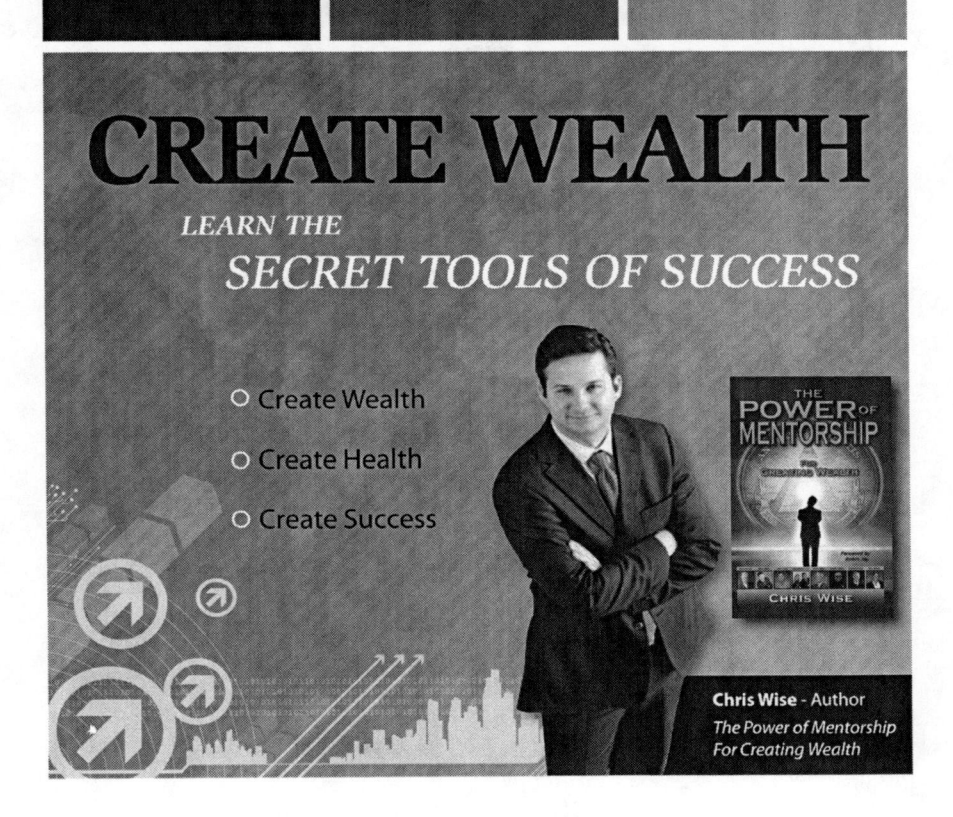

LEARN THE
SECRET TOOLS OF SUCCESS

- Create Wealth
- Create Health
- Create Success

Chris Wise - Author
The Power of Mentorship For Creating Wealth

Free E-Book Version of
"Creating Wealth"

Want to learn more? You can get Chris' free E-Book version of "The Power of Mentorship For Creating Wealth" by going to

www.creditlinemillionaire.com/cash-now

Now you too are about to **learn the secrets** that will give you the tools to create the kind of wealth and success you desire. The only difference between a rich person and a poor person is their method of thinking.

Get Your Free E-Book Today!

THE HOME
SAVERS

NO Credit Check
Bad Credit OK
• Lower the monthly payment
• Results in less than 30 days

Possible Solutions:
• Principle Reduction
• Interest Rate Reduction
• And more

702-995-4824

www.loanfix101.com

Printed in the United States
146220LV00001B/4/P